Todd Haynes |

Contemporary Film Directors

Edited by James Naremore

The Contemporary Film Directors series provides concise, well-written introductions to directors from around the world and from every level of the film industry. Its chief aims are to broaden our awareness of important artists, to give serious critical attention to their work, and to illustrate the variety and vitality of contemporary cinema. Contributors to the series include an array of internationally respected critics and academics. Each volume contains an incisive critical commentary, an informative interview with the director, and a detailed filmography.

A list of books in the series appears at the end of this book.

Todd Haynes |

Rob White

UNIVERSITY OF ILLINOIS PRESS
URBANA, CHICAGO, AND SPRINGFIELD

Frontispiece: Todd Haynes during filming of *I'm Not There,*
courtesy of Todd Haynes.
Images from *Safe* © 1995 The Chemical Films Limited Partnership;
images from *Poison* © 1990 Poison L.P.; image from *Dottie Gets Spanked*
© 1993 Caboose Productions; images from *Velvet Goldmine* © 1998 Velvet
Goldmine Productions Ltd / Newmarket Capital LLC; images from *Far
from Heaven* © 2002 Focus Features LLC / Vulcan Productions Inc.;
images from *I'm Not There* © 2007 VIP Medienfonds 4 GmbH & Co. KG;
image from *Assassins* © 1985 Todd Haynes; images from *Mildred Pierce*
© 2011 Home Box Office Inc.

Library of Congress Cataloging-in-Publication Data
White, Rob, 1970–
Todd Haynes / by Rob White.
p.   cm. — (Contemporary film directors)
Includes bibliographical references and index.
Includes filmography.
ISBN 978-0-252-03756-6 (hardcover : alk. paper) —
ISBN 978-0-252-07910-8 (pbk. : alk. paper) —
ISBN 978-0-252-09481-1 (e-book)
1. Haynes, Todd—Criticism and interpretation. I. Title.
PN1998.3.H385W45   2013
791.4302'33092—dc23   2012032489

Contents |

Acknowledgments |

Thanks to Leo Bersani, Joan Catapano, Joshua Clover, Kelly Gray, Todd Haynes, Marion Hebblethwaite, Dustin Hubbart, David Kaplan, D. A. Miller, Matt Mitchell, Danny Nasset, Joe Peeples, Nina Power, Tad Ringo, Vijay Shah, Mark Sinker, Paul Julian Smith, Tanya Smith, and especially James Naremore.

Todd Haynes |

The Misery the World Is Made Of

The Cinema of Todd Haynes

Prologue

There are moments in Todd Haynes's films when someone is so unnerved that it is difficult to imagine that any good can come from the experience. In *Safe* (1995), Carol White (Julianne Moore) is suddenly distressed while she is talking to her husband: "Oh God, what is this? Where am I? Right now?" It is as if she feels that there is almost nothing left of her as a result of psychic erosion she never knew was occurring. Then, in the five-part miniseries *Mildred Pierce* (2011), the title character played by Kate Winslet is overcome while she listens to her estranged daughter—a piercing, quicksilver coloratura soprano on the cusp of fame—singing an aria by Delibes on the radio. Mildred's face is seized by an expression that first looks like shock and then looks like frozen desperation. After a few moments of glaciation she stumbles away to a jetty nearby, and it is not clear as she stands above the ocean, struggling to breathe, whether the sound of the broadcast that has hurt so much can even still reach her.

Carol in crisis (*Safe*). |

Carol and Mildred are less than they seem. There is something empty about them, an I'm-not-there-ness. They are not safe. In certain circumstances, unprotected, they are more like shadows or ghosts, and their evanescence is linked to Haynes's resistance to naturalism. *Far from Heaven* (2002) is a tapestry woven from the threads of other films—strands of dialogue, character, mise-en-scène—and even briefly ornamented, he explains during the DVD commentary, by an actual piece of scenery from Douglas Sirk's melodrama *Written on the Wind* (1956). *Far from Heaven*'s environment is a patchwork world, with no true identity. Since it is socially regimented and hostile too, the film realm might just as well be called an ingenious dungeon. "I have the impression we are all in prison" (80), wrote the theorist Guy Hocquenghem in his 1973 text *The Screwball Asses*, and *Far from Heaven* conveys something similar, strange though it may seem, given that the setting is Connecticut in 1957–58.

One of the ways in which *Superstar: The Karen Carpenter Story* (1988) violates realistic conventions, apart from using dolls instead of actors, is to have image formats crash together within a single shot, as when a refilmed television clip almost devours another scene of psychic meltdown, this time involving the anorexic singer who has left an oppressive family home only to be even more tormented on her own. Such stylizations depict a whole world of pain, and in my understanding of Haynes's harrowing films, some good does come out of the portrayal—if a sense of how much is wrong can be called good.

Superstar: The Karen Carpenter Story

Disputed Legacy

Haynes got there first, unofficially, but *The Karen Carpenter Story* is also the title of a 1989 TV movie directed by Joseph Sargeant, first broadcast by CBS. After "Rainy Days and Mondays" plays over images of a memento wall of Carpenters photos (altered to contain the faces of the film's actors), a cut reveals the body of Karen (Cynthia Gibb) being attended by medics. A creepy scene at the hospital ensues: the gurney carrying her is a passed by a roller skater, who turns out to be the singer as a teenager, magically transported into the future. She looks down mildly at her dying older self before skating off back to 1960s California, where the main narrative begins. In a later scene, the Carpenter matriarch Agnes (Louise Fletcher) tells a therapist that she does not "put much stock in this psychiatry business," and it makes sense that the TV film doubles Karen in the hospital: it is a way of getting at the idea that she was broken in some way without suggesting either psychic split or damaging home environment.

Richard Carpenter, Karen's brother and bandmate, was the executive producer (and the Internet Movie Database names him as uncredited codirector) of Sargeant's film, and it reflects the family's stance that Karen's death was either genetic or inexplicable. Writing for *TV Guide* in 1988, Richard stated: "She would have suffered the same problem even if she were a homemaker." And elsewhere: "I have no answers. People have been trying to get that out of me. If I had it, I'd give it" (qtd. in Schmidt 7–8). Interviewed by Richard Dyer at London's Tate Modern on June 4, 2004, Haynes explained *Superstar* as a challenge to this vague orthodoxy: "We wanted to redeem Karen Carpenter's image and felt that she was a victim of not only an eating disorder, but an incredibly . . . invasive family drama. . . . Even in death she was still being controlled by her family . . . and it just seemed like there was no escape, and we wanted to do our little movie out of a desire to make you cry for Karen."

If different ways of posthumously telling the late superstar's story involve a clash between family values and psychological trauma—between roller skates and gurney—then the former wins out in *The Karen Carpenter Story*. A telling scene occurs just after Karen has admitted her fantasy of family to Richard (Mitchell Anderson). ("I'm gonna find somebody who just wants me," she murmurs. "I can just see it now. I'll have the cottage in Connecticut, and the station wagon and the kids, and my husband will wear those plaid flannel shirts.") It is summer 1974: the siblings visit the house they have bought for their parents before Karen announces, to Agnes's dismay, that she will not be moving into the room Agnes has prepared for her. Her usually taciturn father, Harold (Peter Michael Goetz), replies: "I think if you took a look at the room your mother fixed up for you, you'll find there aren't any bars on the window." Imprisonment (and worse) is, however, precisely what *Superstar* insists on.

The Carpenters' music itself complicates these matters, especially when it combines frustrated romantic yearning with jubilant instrumentation. The epitome of this uneasy mix is "Goodbye to Love," composed by Richard, who was inspired by a song that is named but never heard in the Bing Crosby film *Rhythm on the River* (dir. Victor Schertzinger, 1940), together with John Bettis. It is an early instance of a pop power ballad and the first to include ecstatic "fuzztone" guitar solos (by Tony Peluso). "Goodbye to Love," true to its title, professes (with a hint of Christian piety) the abandonment of Eros, but it is an assertive abandonment in which forsaking becomes a perverse form of companionship that is cherished not only in the lyrics—"Loneliness and empty days will be my only friend"—but also in Karen's singing, which builds in energy until, ushered in by celebratory backing vocals, the distorted electric guitar realizes the underlying exultation . . . as if this were after all a love song and not a renunciation song. Given its triumphalism, does "Goodbye to Love" truly relinquish desire, as its words purport? Better to say that the erotic abstinence is itself tragically passionate.

"Goodbye to Love" suggests not an absence but a crisis of desire—and thus implies the anorexia nervosa that would kill Karen. "Anorexia" means "without appetite," but what is involved in the illness is a fierce and sometimes unstoppable dedication, an addiction, a tormented appetite for appetitelessness, not any feeble habit of omission. Since Richard constructed the Carpenters' music, it might be tempting to imagine a form of sibling rivalry and make a distinction between his flamboyant musical arrangements and Karen's vocal melancholy, between extravagance and sadness, but it was Karen who lived out the entire ardent drama of renunciation to a fatal limit.

Home Front

It is February 4, 1983 (according to a title card), and Karen is found by her mother sprawled on the carpet: "*Karen!* Oh God—HARRY!! Harry—it's Karen! Oh God . . . HARRY!!" Agnes's desperate cries repetitively stitch the names together just at the moment when the family has been torn apart. With a menacingly slow touch of pastiche in his voice, an offscreen male narrator intervenes: "What happened? Why, at the age of thirty-two, was this smooth-voiced girl from Downey, California, who led a raucous nation smoothly into the seventies, found dead in her parents' home?" Mixing up the mode of sensationalist TV documentary with the flashback storytelling of such classical Hollywood crime films as *Mildred Pierce* (1945) and *Sunset Blvd.* (1950—"Let's go back about six months and find the day when it all started"), which both open with murder scenes, Haynes's narrator summons the story away from the corpse and into the past—"Let's go back, back to southern California, where Karen and Richard grew up"—and as he does so, the dead singer's yearning voice rises up with its own agenda of reminiscence.

"Long ago, and oh so far away," she sings in a fragment of "Superstar," as the opening titles appear over a traveling shot of suburban homes. This song, originally entitled "Groupie," was written by Leon Russell and Bonnie Bramlett and first performed by Rita Coolidge (and later Bette Midler): a groupie listens to the radio, hears music by the rock star she has spent a night with, and longs to "sleep with" him again. In the Carpenters' version, the chart-friendly "be with you again" is substituted for "sleep with you again"; bouncy layers of backing vocals and even trumpets reinforce the makeover. The sexual frankness is, in an ordinary showbiz way, censored—again renounced. But this time, especially in the song's intro (oboe, strings, French horns) and the way Karen sings the plaintive first verse, a profound desolation and sorrow can be heard, without any trace of euphoria or dutifulness, the exhausted sadness of someone who has drifted far out to sea and can only look in despair at the faint lights of human habitation on shore that she will never get back to.

Superstar recounts the Carpenters' stellar career in snappy scenes and mini-music-video montages. Hearing Karen singing to herself at home one day, it is Agnes who suggests to the more precociously musical Richard that his sister would make the perfect bandmate. The duo is soon signed to A&M: "You kids are young and fresh, and it'll just be up to us to make young and fresh a happening thing." As it proceeds, punctuated by voiceovers from the lugubrious male heard at the beginning and then a second, female narrator, *Superstar* intersperses such sitcom-like accelerated storytelling with more title cards that parody health-information campaigns, flashes of archival footage, and jokey talking-head commentary. The way the scene in the record-company office continues is typical of the film's stylistic amalgam. The character called Mr. A&M (Herb Alpert, the label's cofounder, signed the group) closes the deal by saying, "All you have to do is put yourself in my hands." Then, as the script puts it, "*Music and intercutting between* KAREN *and* MR. A&M *build as a shadowy, slow-motion close-up of a human hand moving ominously toward a handshake takes over his final line.*" The sound track turns sinister again as the storytelling yields to nonnarrative imagery: the character's trust-me speech is slowed and distorted before a woman's screaming takes over as the grisly, disembodied hand points the way to a "*black-and-white Holocaust image of an emaciated female carcass being thrown into a pit.*" Again horror intrudes, suddenly revealing a terrible dimension adjoining the lighthearted biopic episodes. A lengthy card borrows from radical feminist theory's account of the cruelty of both psychic and domestic interiority: "As we investigate the story of Karen Carpenter's life and death we are presented with an extremely graphic picture of the internal experience of contemporary femininity. We will see how Karen's visibility as a popular singer only intensified certain difficulties many women experience in relation to their bodies."

Fame and success follow swiftly for the siblings: hits, TV appearances, awards. The narrator situates the group's astonishing career (by 1981, A&M had sold seventy-nine million Carpenters singles and LPs) in terms of its feel-good repudiation of youth rebellion: "The year is 1970, and suddenly the nation finds itself asking the question: what if, instead of the riots and assassinations, the protests and the drugs, instead of the angry words and hard-rock sounds, we were to hear something soft and smooth, and see something of wholesomeness and easy-handed faith." It is a time of triumph and celebrity, but the horizon darkens as Karen begins to obsess about her appearance. "You have just been so fanatical about your weight," Agnes says. "I just want to start watching what I eat," Karen replies. Karen eats less and less, and starts using laxatives to slim down. In 1973 the Carpenters sing for Richard Nixon at the White House.

Various personages, including the DJ Todd Donovan (played in wrap-around sunglasses by Haynes), debate the group's music in another interlude. A card notes Karen's friendship with such luminaries as Dionne Warwick and Olivia Newton-John, but adds: "It was the inner relationship with herself that dominated Karen's life." Richard implores her to eat more during a tour, but she is oblivious. More cards theorize the existence of "a complex internal apparatus of resistance and control," propounding a catastrophic dramaturgy of anorexia: "an addiction and abuse of self-control, a fascism over the body in which the sufferer plays the parts of both dictator and the emaciated victim." The world war inside Karen is reaching a crisis. One day in Las Vegas, Richard finds her passed out in her dressing room. He berates her—"What are you trying to do, ruin *both* our careers?"—and she starts to cry. Later, Karen collapses onstage. She wakes up in the hospital.

Nearing her twenty-fifth birthday, having apparently recovered, Karen announces to her reluctant parents that she is moving to a condo in Century City. She holds a housewarming party and proudly shows off her huge TV set, but in the next scene Richard furiously confronts her when he finds laxatives again. Karen counters calmly and mysteriously: "I'll tell . . . about you and your—*private* life!"

When she is home alone later, hallucinatory hectoring voices overwhelm her. The camera work is jittery, stoned; "Superstar" can be heard again, but its miserable words are muffled and distorted now, as if emanating from behind the wall of a padded cell. Karen's condo has become a haunted, alien home, not the refuge she hoped it would be. The disintegrating vocal also loops back on itself: "Long ago, and oh so far away" echoes again, the song unable to move forward, as if it were itself stuck in a room, lost in darkness and limbo time. Karen stumbles, filmed from a low angle, while the visuals fragment deliriously and chaotically. *Superstar* is nothing other than a horror film now. An infestation of what the script calls "strange, belated images" crowds out Karen from the screen. She is thus eaten away audiovisually—as a protagonist, she no longer holds her own against the onslaught of clips. Replicating the way the contorted singing repeats, these invading images—a plate with food that looks like a fluorescent bacillus, a doll-spanking scene shot from above, bodies falling or being dragged, a Partridge Family performance, and another screen showing only jagged electronic feedback—recur to increase the impression of trauma and fracture.

In the middle of this nightmare montage, Karen sits . . . eating. Behind her, huge, is that same wholesome TV dance routine. It is not playing on the trophy set in the corner but fills the whole background in the fashion of a cinematic rear projection. Indicative of *Superstar*'s whole approach, a clip that should epitomize family-friendly pop culture becomes a monstrous threat; the rescaled TV set is transformed from a square of entertainment in the corner of a room to an outsized vortex devouring domestic space, as if the side of the apartment had been silently ripped off without Karen noticing it to reveal an encroaching parallel universe out of *The Time Tunnel* or *Poltergeist* (dir. Tobe Hooper, 1982). Simultaneously a chorus of persecution builds: "What are you doing with these? . . . I was constipated. . . . Oh, you LIAR! . . . Why can't she find a nice place in Downey? Why does she have to be out in the middle of . . . ? All you have to do is put yourself in my hands. . . . You have just been so fanatical about your weight. . . . All you ever eat is salad and iced tea. . . . What are you trying to do, ruin both our careers? . . . That thing really went to your head. . . . Do the Carpenters have something to hide?" The voices of Agnes, Richard, and Mr. A&M knot together in a clamor. Karen has become a kind of ventriloquists' dummy, a host for treacherous parasitic voices; much of the pathos of *Superstar* has to do with the idea that the Karen who might have been able to voice reasons, griefs, and sorrows had begun disappearing long ago, even before she started to starve her flesh away. There is a subjective as well as a corporeal erosion, and what is eaten away makes space for these rattling fragments of other people's opinions, taunts, and demands. They blow through this nightmare room like the wind through motheaten cloth.

The dreadful crisis somehow passes. Karen's subsequent marriage in 1980 to Tom Burris fails quickly. (As this doomed union is recounted, the song "Masquerade" plays over ghostly footage of a masked woman from the 1943 Julien Duvivier portmanteau film *Flesh and Fantasy*.) Richard continues to remonstrate about Karen's failure to eat. Squaring up to the issue, she does seek treatment in New York (with the help of Cherry Boone O'Neill, the author of *Starving for Attention: A Young Woman's Struggle and Triumph over Anorexia Nervosa,* and a doctor called Steven Levenkron). The hit single that accompanies the New York montage—including taxicabs, an ominous box of Ex-Lax pills, Radio City Music Hall, and Karen on the therapist's couch—is "For All We Know," a song for newlyweds adapted from the schmaltzy wedding ditty in the 1970 film *Lovers and Other Strangers*—as if some happy future were in view for Karen. Yet the image in the sequence that really counts is the one showing Karen hurriedly striding with needless vigor. Her healthy-seeming journeys to and from therapy are in effect a way of controlling her weight through exertion rather than self-starvation. Less overtly horrifying than other moments in *Superstar,* this image is nonetheless one of self-destruction. What should signify convalescence instead has to be understood as an image of death working out.

Karen seems to rally, and when she returns to California, the Carpenter family eats a meal she has cooked. A closeup of vomit-causing Ipecac syrup indicates that there has been no recovery. Carpenters songs and alarm sounds converge cacophonously, and the superstar, plagued by terrors and secret desires, dies on the bedroom floor.

Star Studies

Superstar's depiction of a doomed performer connects it to films in both the Hollywood and European traditions, and to an idea expressed by Haynes in a video introduction to the Criterion edition of Max Ophuls's *Le Plaisir* (1952): "There's this cost to the spectacle, there's this cost to the beauty and the excess and the profusion of these realms that we're seeing." Consider a scene in *The Bad and the Beautiful,* Vincente Minnelli's behind-the-silver-screen melodrama (told through flashbacks), also from 1952. The mercurial mogul Jonathan Shields (Kirk Douglas) visits the actress Georgia Lorrison (Lana Turner) as she boozes in a rented room. He castigates her for being "haunted, born to live by make-believe." She simpers, and this eggs him on. "The cheap performance of a bit player, not a star! And that's all it'll ever be until you can pull yourself out of this tomb! Until you can see people as they really are, yourself as you really are!" (Charles Schnee's lively writing here is true to the film's high-spirited take on thespian wretchedness, but later in the film something much more extreme briefly takes over: Georgia flees Jonathan's mansion after she has found him with another woman and drives away frantically in a rainstorm, howling and screaming with pain, arms waving around as if she were being convulsed by electric shocks.)

Other American forerunners include a series of anti-psychiatric dramas such as *Bigger Than Life* (dir. Nicholas Ray, 1956), *Shock Corridor* (dir. Samuel Fuller, 1963), and *Suddenly, Last Summer* (dir. Joseph L. Mankiewicz, 1959), whose deceased poet is described as having been "half-starved from living on pills and salad." Closer still to *Superstar* are martyred-by-illness melodramas such as the Bette Davis vehicle *Dark Victory* (dir. Edmund Goulding, 1939), in which the central character succumbs valiantly to a brain tumor shortly after marrying her doctor, plaintively demanding of him as she expires to confirm that she has been a good wife. Another Davis film, *Now, Voyager* (dir. Irving Rapper, 1942), shares *Superstar*'s emphases on maternal unkindness ("Dr. Jaquith says that tyranny is sometimes an expression of the maternal instinct") and erratic eating, which is discussed in relation to an adolescent girl, about whom a nurse comments: "Don't be disturbed if you hear her crying. She has spells of it. Just ignore it. It's one of her little tyrannies, like refusing to eat. Just ignore that too, or if you could manage to get a little food into her tonight, it would help." (These films, preoccupied by female subservience and the honorable authority of the medical profession, are the subject of a book by Mary Ann Doane, with whom Haynes studied at Brown, *The Desire to Desire*.) The theme of unusual eating habits also crops up in another Mankiewicz work, *Dragonwyck* (1946). A woman dies, causing her doctor to think out loud before he curtails the thought: "I don't know why she died. That's shameful, isn't it? For a doctor not to know. It's funny the way she ate . . . almost passionately, as if she wanted from eating what she couldn't have. . . ."

Superstar has an affinity with Ophuls's *La signora di tutti* (1934), which begins with the scratchy sound of a recording of the *signora's* trademark lament: "I am in everyone's heart / But I am very sad, / I am the love of the world / Nobody is for me." At the end of the first sequence, the film star–chanteuse is found collapsed on a bathroom floor before the film goes back in time, like Haynes's film does, to chart her downfall. Another point of comparison is Rainer Werner Fassbinder's *Veronika Voss* (1982). It begins in a mode familiar from *Sunset Blvd.*, with an impecunious former idol latching on to a somewhat bewildered journalist, but then suddenly becomes something scarier when Veronika (Rosel Zech) turns out to be in thrall to morphine administered by the malevolent director (Annemarie Düringer) of a private psychiatric clinic. "She comes here in cases of emergency," the clinician says, "when the pain becomes unbearable." And Veronika is dangerous to those around her, according to her ex-husband (Armin Mueller-Stahl), who utters a grim warning: "She'll destroy you because she's a lost soul, because she's an addict."

In *Gaslight* (dir. George Cukor, 1944), a Hollywood picture Europeanized by the casting of Ingrid Bergman and Charles Boyer and on account of being an adaptation of Patrick Hamilton's stage play, a former opera singer is driven to the brink of insanity by her scheming, murderous husband. He deceives and manipulates her until she starts to believe that she is hallucinating; but *Gaslight* never suggests that perception and reality may indeed have started to separate, that the world has started to become unrecognizable. This disturbing epistemological break is exactly what *Superstar* considers, especially in the cacophonous nighttime condo scene, in which Karen and the confined space around her descend into the chaos of a tangled mesh of competing sounds and images. The scene recalls the transformation in Roman Polanski's *Repulsion* (1965) of a neat London home: as Carole (Catherine Deneuve) goes mad, the mansion flat she shares with her sister becomes a surreal charnel house. The dimensions of the space change: it grows larger as it gets more fetid and bloody, the walls cracking and demon limbs emerging to clutch Carole. The apparitions, vile descendants of the ceremonious arms in Jean Cocteau's *Beauty and the Beast* (1946), are creatures of her insanity, but nothing exactly demarcates the separate territory of delirium. Whereas in *Gaslight* reality is made unsafe and hard to know only because of purposeful deception, in *Repulsion* and the *Superstar* apartment scene, reality itself is a kind of madness.

During the condo crisis, Karen's psychic coherence, relations to family, and domestic environment all disintegrate. And in the process the singer suffers a loss of voice as part of the scene's calamitous sonic disturbances: sound is used to express abjection, identity breakdown, and cognitive shock. There is a link between this aspect of *Superstar* and auditory hallucinations that occur in other films. In the gloomy old mansion in *Dragonwyck,* a little girl hears a spectral singing at night; in *La signora di tutti,* the woman who will soon become a tragic idol swoons with crushing shame and despondency, believing she has just heard the music that played when another woman died nearby. The film that *Superstar* most resembles in this respect (and which also conjures up *Repulsion*) is one that could not have influenced it, Darren Aronofsky's *Black Swan* (2010), especially the brief scene in which the disturbed, self-injuring ballet dancer (Natalie Portman) enters her mother's room and is confronted by expressionistic portraits that start to move, manically repeating the phrases "sweet girl" and "my turn."

Barbification

Superstar uses dolls in the place of human actors. In his study of the film, Glyn Davis links this to screen puppetry. But a doll is not exactly a puppet, especially when, as in *Superstar,* it never approximates actual human movement (moving arms, mouths, and so on), even in the ridiculous fashion of the Gerry Anderson "Supermarionation" TV series mentioned by Davis, *Captain Scarlet* and *Thunderbirds.* An animated model, manually operated puppet, or other similar mechanical contraption is to some degree lifelike in its movement, whereas a stiffly posed doll that occasionally wobbles or shifts clumsily to the side or is lifted up into the frame, though anthropomorphic, more eerily suggests the unliving and the inhuman. The dolls in *Superstar,* never subject to a technique like stop-motion animation, are not really like puppets, let alone people. These objects are better described as deathlike than lifelike—semblances from which life is absolutely absent rather than effigies that animatronics can seem to revitalize, even if only robotically. It may look a little like someone, as waxworks do, yet a doll is a mockery of a person. This is especially the case of the Agnes doll in *Superstar,* whose visage is monstrous, as if diseased or decomposing and resembling (as has often been noted) the mummified maternal corpse in *Psycho* (dir. Alfred Hitchcock, 1960).

The "feeling like I don't belong" that is expressed in the Carpenters song "Rainy Days and Mondays," the feeling of not having a place in the world or vanishing from it, losing shape and substance, is sometimes expressed in films. In *Cutter and Bone* (dir. Ivan Passer, 1981), for example, a woman murmurs: "When I wake up in the night alone, and I can't sleep, I have to go and look and see if I'm still there." This is, however, not a malaise that easily lends itself to visualization. How to depict a fading away, the slow emaciation of the self? *Superstar's* condo scene finds one acoustic solution: Karen's recorded voice is abbreviated and deformed, making room for hostile other voices that displace her so that her presence is drastically diminished. But the use of dolls is Haynes's main solution—albeit a paradoxical one, because of the doll's rigid physicality—to this problem of representation. The dolls in *Superstar* are just these plastic things from which all human traits are *missing*: desire, thought, even those characteristics that make a face truly a face—expressive movement and constant aging. Perhaps the gross, even obscene presence of these lifeless objects is an almost mythopoeic way of imagining the spectral evaporation of being and the slow annihilation of the psyche as a process of calcification, or rather plastification. The person slowly seizes up, gradually petrified, until there is nothing left of her except this carapace-like casing made of chemicals.

Superstar includes a brief, black-and-white, closeup clip from *Flesh and Fantasy* of a woman wearing a blank-faced mask. No thematic connection is obvious between Haynes's horror biopic and the redemptive love story, the first episode in Duvivier's film. The episode is set during Mardi Gras in New Orleans: Henrietta (Betty Field), a bitter Cinderella, frustrated in love because of her "homely" face, wears a mask that gives her the confidence to seduce the man she desires. When she takes off the "mask of selfishness" at midnight, her coiffure and makeup (now flatteringly lit) have been miraculously transformed, and she is a beauty after all! One of the film's compères spells it out: "I think the mask is just supposed to tell the moral of the story: that faith in yourself is the main thing."

The clip lasts for just a few seconds. Transplanted, no dialogue can be heard, and no redemptive arc moralizes the masked face. A viewer cannot listen to the pleading words that are in fact being spoken by Henrietta at this juncture in the narrative: "Oh, Michael, don't throw away your whole future. All the hard work you've given to it—it would be like putting an end to yourself." While "Masquerade" plays, the viewer of *Superstar* sees only refilmed, poor-quality images of a woman pulling back from what seems to be an embrace, separating herself, her face obscured by the porcelanic encrustation formed by the mask. This flash of *Flesh and Fantasy* thus works like other ghostly distortions in *Superstar,* and works against its source. Relocated, the fleetingly glimpsed woman with her sickly, shining visage appears, in direct contradiction of the unheard plea for self-assertion she is invisibly speaking from behind her mask's molded lips, to be withdrawing from the world and relinquishing the future in the process of putting an end to herself—the process of becoming a deathlike doll. The actual, original narrative and message of *Flesh and Fantasy* is affirmative, hopeful, morally wholesome—as the Carpenters' music was often perceived to be ("Young America at its very best," as Nixon said at the White House on May 1, 1973). Excerpted like this, though, *Flesh and Fantasy*'s optimistic and compliant message is silenced, and what is left is like a horrifying X-ray that reveals the skull beneath the skin, the mask beneath the person. In betraying *Flesh and Fantasy,* the clip sums up *Superstar.*

Supersad

Throughout Haynes's film, audiovisual distortion and especially uncanny juxtapositions, overlaps, tangles, and loops open up a dimension of horror and trauma at the level of the film's form. Thus clips of real human bodies displace film of dolls, with the added dimension that the clips are mutilated, having often been played from a VHS tape on a TV screen and then refilmed on 16mm, and so the way they offset the dolls is itself offset by the element of distancing the clips share with the dolls. One kind of distortion meets another—and in a curious way, the factor of depersonalization may actually be more pronounced in the clips of real people because whereas the dolls are unavoidably solid-seeming, the clips fizz and flicker as if their power supply were intermittent and thus appear (as the dolls mostly do not) subject to a process of emaciation. As Lucas Hilderbrand argued in "Grainy Days and Mondays," form starts to replicate content: the film's "thematic concerns—mass-media distortion and its relations to subjective and bodily breakdown—become rendered on the surface" (61). When the black-and-white Holocaust clips appear, or monochrome film of Nixon from a time before *Superstar*'s events occur, the sudden presence of a disjointed history—the long-ago, the oh-so-far-away—adds another dimension of instability and uncertainty, time itself fragmenting.

After it was withdrawn from exhibition in 1989 (having had more than a year of festival and metropolitan success) at the insistence of the songs' copyright-holders, the film began a subcultural afterlife as a bootleg VHS. This accident of exhibition increased the text's on-the-surface pathos: as one tape was copied and then that tape in turn copied, the audiovisual quality continued to worsen. More scuffing, more eerie fading away, like lichen cracking a windswept tombstone. This version of Karen's story slipped more out of reach; she drifted further out to sea. But this meant, in Hilderbrand's analysis of *Superstar*'s pirate existence, that fans could renew and intensify their love for the lost object: "Analog reproduction of the text, rather than destroying the original's aura, actually reconstructs it. Materially, the fallout of the image and the sound mark each successive copy as an illicit object, a forbidden pleasure watched and shared and loved to exhaustion" (71). The new cycle of degradation paradoxically reenergized spectatorial desire and, furthermore, convened a small, reverent congregation, a group constituted like the scattered members of a persecuted church by the web of transactions as a result of which one tape bequeathed another. Hilderbrand surveyed *Superstar* fans for his article and found that the experience of seeing or acquiring the film was often itself poignantly memorable, so that watching the film soon could start to inspire nostalgia for the event of its duplication, purchase, or previous screening. Thus the process of fragmentation that bootlegging visibly exacerbates is paradoxically compensated for socially. The terrible becoming-nothing that *Superstar* depicts, the lostness and hauntedness that overtake Karen in the film, are ameliorated by the devotion of the fans' accidental nostalgic community. Even the bootlegged text's visual decay gains a new redemptive dimension because "every duplication has a unique effect on the transfer, so that each printed cassette becomes a singular text that contains and compounds its circulatory history" (78). Each tape becomes a relic, a rag from the shroud, turning every viewing into a gratifying ritual of commemoration.

Until, that is, VHS bootlegging was superseded by digital piracy and

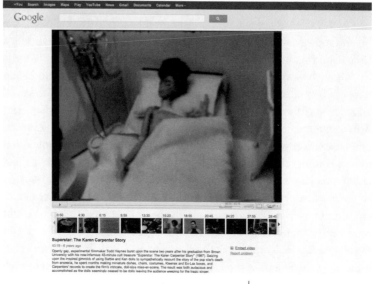

Superstar online.

the Internet's far more impersonal system of unauthorized distribution, the system that allows *Superstar* to be viewed in its entirety on Google Video, and which transforms Haynes's film again. In a way, miniaturized in a browser window, *Superstar* becomes a drained replica of itself. Whichever version may at any given time be viewable online is now divested, even though it is likely to be an encoding of an originally bootlegged copy, of the aura and tactility of the pirate tape that was formerly passed fondly, fervently between friends and dealers. There for all to see on the computer screen is *Superstar,* this dark story of breakdown, desire in crisis, domestic horror, and the cost of the spectacle, the pathos of all its surface abrasions still visible. Yet is it the same sad text, surrounded—dolled up—by all the Web-page paraphernalia of controller, logos, search boxes, links to other videos? Its anguish in this setting is ossified. Encased in a plasticky white border decorated with corporate badges, *Superstar* suffers a fate worse than degradation and bootlegging: it becomes almost banal. Looking at *Superstar* in its Google dollhouse, the latest sadness of this terribly sad film is that all its sadness should have come to this.

Poison

Against the Norm

What is queer about Haynes's first feature, in which sex between males is bullying intercourse taking place in Borstal or prison, reported role-play among schoolboys, or (if this indeed counts as sex) spanking? In 1992, B. Ruby Rich defined the New Queer Cinema that *Poison* pioneered as "homo pomo," involving "appropriation and pastiche, irony, as well as reworking of history with social constructionism very much in mind." These films are "irreverent, energetic, alternately minimalist and excessive"—and, she added, "they're full of pleasure" (16). Perhaps surprisingly, given its evident though indirect concern with the AIDS epidemic, it is true that *Poison* is witty and playful, but it builds to an intense pathos. Characters die abjectly, and the way Haynes braids the storylines together accentuates the negative. Thus playfulness is over-taken by the sorrow that an influential 1989 essay by Douglas Crimp, "Mourning and Militancy," argued had been suppressed among AIDS activists: "There is no question but that we must fight the unspeakable violence we incur from the society in which we find ourselves. But if we understand that violence is able to reap its horrible rewards through the very psychic mechanisms that make us part of this society, then we may be able to recognize—along with our rage—our terror, our guilt, and our profound sadness. Militancy, of course, then, but mourning too: mourning and militancy" (18). Yet if *Poison*'s grief is unmistakable, it is also complicated by the film's conclusion, in which something much larger than a character is killed off. Of the New Queer characteristics identified by Rich, it is minimalism that ultimately dominates. There is nothing left at the end.

Interviewed by Justin Wyatt for the Summer 1993 *Film Quarterly*, Haynes said: "I have a lot of frustration with the insistence on content when people are talking about homosexuality. People define gay cinema solely by content: if there are gay characters in it, it's a gay film. It fits into the gay sensibility, we got it, it's gay. It's such a failure of the imagination, let alone the ability to look beyond content. I think that's really simplistic. Heterosexuality to me is a structure as much as it is a content. It is an imposed structure that goes along with the patriarchal, dominant structure that constrains and defines society. If homosexuality is the opposite or the counter-sexual activity to that, then what kind of a structure would it be?" And he added: "For me it's the way . . . that films are machines that either reiterate and reciprocate society—or not" (8). What in *Poison*'s style is antisocial, nonreciprocal? What is unconstrained, resists confinement? If pastiche, irreverence, and the knitted, multilinear storytelling are certainly part of the queer practice of dissent, it should be noted that the last element in particular involves a sort of gregariousness in the way it brings characters together. But the onscreen absence and then flight of the child protagonist of the "Hero" storyline perform a vanishing act that more completely refuses society.

Poison explores a difference between coming out and getting out. To come out is to affirm as legitimate—and so to demand acceptance of—a presence, especially a homosexual presence in the world and more particularly in families; it is to refuse the closet, to insist on visibility, and the history of AIDS activism shows how important the demand can be. The spirit of such activism animates a remark that the actor and playwright Harvey Fierstein makes in the documentary *The Celluloid Closet* (dirs. Rob Epstein and Jeffrey Friedman, 1996): "My view has always been: visibility at any cost. I'd rather have negative than nothing." But visibility is also dangerous and entrapping. Near the finale of *Poison,* law enforcers track down the fugitive, infected scientist, Dr. Thomas Graves (Larry Maxwell). "This time we have you completely surrounded, and there is no chance of escape," the Centerville County deputy shouts through a bullhorn. "You are ordered to make yourself visible!" *Poison* also abounds with less official scenes of social censure: gossiping, gawking, harassing. It starts to seem like the whole of social space were coercive such that the truest rebellion is—if it can be done—to get out altogether. As the queer theorist Leo Bersani succinctly put it in *Homos*: "I can't be oppressed if I can't be found" (32).

Championing visible homosexuality meets the difficulty that social tolerance, especially in the area of sex, may be a more effective form of domination than prohibition. It was Michel Foucault, writing in the first volume of *The History of Sexuality,* who cautioned against what he termed the "repressive hypothesis" that Victorian morality had sought to block and proscribe sexual behavior other than conjugal, preferably reproductive intercourse. On the contrary, Foucault claimed, Victorians assiduously discussed, confessed, categorized, medicalized, and penalized sex, which had previously been a capricious realm of experience that to a large extent evaded discourse: "Sex became something to say" (32); "A censorship of sex? There was installed rather an apparatus for producing an ever greater quantity of discourse about sex" (33). Far from marginalizing sexuality and especially the fruitless kind, the process framed sexuality—even created it in the process of designating it aberrant or pathological—lest otherwise it stay "clandestine" (66) and thus outside the range of what Foucault called "biopower," defined as "numerous and diverse techniques for achieving the subjugation of bodies and the control of populations" (140). The techniques of this minimum-force regime encourage participation from those subjected to its covert domination. Biopower develops institutions that manage to enlist the collusion of their occupants: medicine, education, family— hospital, high school, home. Proliferating sex discourse sets sex in a clamp rather than shutting it out. The nuclear family restricts certain behaviors only after first having thrown a punitive spotlight on them— like a stray cat dragged into a house for the express purpose of being strangled in front of the children. By this logic, to come out in order to obtain recognition and safety within the family is an act of compliance that gives up on getting out.

Exploitation Film

Poison's three interwoven storylines deal with outsiders and their lovers. The black-and-white "Horror" begins when police arrive at a boarding house in which a woman is slumped dead. A man escapes through a window as the cops break in, and his story is then told in narrated flashback: "Ever since he was a child, Thomas Graves had been hungry for knowledge, hungry to discover all the secrets of the universe. Science, man's sacred quest for truth, was his first and only love. Years of hard work and research led him to the mysteries of the sex drive and its potential for the betterment of mankind." At age thirty-two he presents his theory that extracted hormones can prevent "paralysis as we know it today" to a roomful of specialists, only to be denounced as incompetent by a distinguished medic. He continues his lab work regardless. There comes a "eureka!" moment: "Putrefacted condensation sustained allowing molecular coagulation by producing biomolecular gas—I did it!" At the moment he sums up his achievement—"I've just captured the sex drive!"—Dr. Nancy Olsen (Susan Gayle Norman) strides in and proclaims her jubilation at finally meeting the man who inspired her doctoral research and wholly reconfigured her understanding of "conditional bioflavenoid neuropathology." The fresh-faced Graves looks almost bewildered by his starstruck visitor; agitated, aroused, he drinks the libidinal distillation instead of his tea, and the next morning, queasy, he checks his body for signs of illness.

During the DVD commentary, Haynes acknowledges several sources of inspiration for the "dank, cheesy" look of "Horror." One of these is Fuller's films. After Graves inadvertently swallows the serum, there is an odd moment when Nancy, who has just walked out, reappears in her former position opposite the celebrating scientist. This time-lapse insert was borrowed directly from *The Naked Kiss* (1964), Fuller's characteristically off-the-wall tale about a prostitute, Kelly (Constance Towers), trying to start a new small-town life only to find herself engaged to a child molester, J. L. (Michael Dante), whom she bludgeons to death with a telephone when she discovers his predilection. Just before she does so, the man is briefly thrilled by the idea that she might accept him: "Now you know why I could never marry a normal woman. That's why I love you. You understand my sickness. You've been conditioned to people like me. You live in my world, and it will be an exciting world. My darling, our marriage will be a paradise because we're both abnormal!" This same idea of romance between two lowlives is expressed with less brutal consequences in *Underworld USA* (1961), by another streetwise woman, Cuddles (Dolores Dorn): "We got a right to climb out of the sewer and live like other people. We could start from scratch, make every minute count twice for the one we lost. . . . I want your kids, Tolly. I want you for my—my husband." Tolly (Cliff Robertson) replies rather unkindly: "You must be on the needle." The fringe world of Fuller's films is dangerous and often criminal—sex crimes, heroin—and within its confines a conventional romanticism (emphasizing marriage in these instances) seems unfamiliar, even transgressive. This applies also to the love affair in "Horror," which is genuinely touching: the polite ardor that characterizes the lethal attraction between Nancy and the morbidly named Graves is an unusual case in Haynes's work of romantic happiness.

Also influential were two low-budget "psychotronic" exploitation movies, *Glen or Glenda* (dir. Edward D. Wood Jr., 1953) and *Carnival of Souls* (dir. Herk Hervey, 1962). In Wood's film, framed by first a cameo performance by Bela Lugosi and then a preposterously earnest health-information-style conversation between a cop and a doctor that includes such lines as "Glen is a transvestite but not a homosexual," a cross-dresser (played under the pseudonym Daniel Davis by Wood himself) confesses to his wife and is reconciled with society. *Carnival of Souls* is eerie rather than camp. A woman emerges shaken from a car wreck. It turns out that she actually died in the accident, but for much of the film she shifts between troubled presence in the world and wraithlike fadeout: "It was as though for a time I didn't exist, as though I had no place in the world, no part of the life around me," she says. The film powerfully conveys, within its limited means, life on an urban fringe of cheap boarding houses and rundown fairgrounds, and at the end its extreme high-angle shots portray city space as an abyss and a hunting ground. "Horror" is less trashily shambolic than either *Glen or Glenda* or *Carnival of Souls,* and it is never plain weird. For a while it is lighthearted—and sweethearted—rather than cranky; then it is deeply disheartened and much more tragic than trash ought to be.

At McGovern's bar, Graves knocks the booze back, lost in unhappy thought, a scaly lesion starting to form at the side of his mouth. The unsightly symptom does not deter a vampish woman who kisses him hungrily and is immediately afflicted by an even worse disfigurement that quickly spreads over her face and then kills her. "LEPER SEX KILLER ON THE LOOSE" is the headline of the *Centerville Sentinel.* He is dejected by the time Nancy calls out of the blue, bubbly and solicitous, and then pounds on his apartment door to find him gripped by self-loathing and disfigured by slimy facial sores. She is only disconcerted for a moment, however, even when, in a canted shot in front of a mirror, he points out that "the hormonal system is self-perpetuating, the biomagnetic field is irreversible. I'm a monster." Any dismay she feels is swept away by tenderness: "It doesn't disgust me in the slightest. On the contrary, it breaks my heart." She hugs him and nestles on his chest.

As they walk down the street, Nancy smiles despite hostile stares, while Graves hides behind big sunglasses. A girl spits in his face. They eat hot dogs at a sidewalk table, maliciously observed by passersby, and Graves's infected forehead drips onto his lunch. (Nancy thinks nothing of it and wipes him down.) Haynes explains during the commentary that this scene is indebted to Fassbinder's *Ali: Fear Eats the Soul* (1974), recalling a meal the eponymous Moroccan immigrant worker, Ali (El Hedi ben Salem), and his older German wife, Emmi (Brigitte Mira), have at an Italian restaurant. The waiter coldly embarrasses the newlyweds when Emmi gets confused about aperitifs and how the Chateaubriand should be cooked.

When Nancy tracks Graves to McGovern's, where he is drinking alone, she earnestly insists that "we belong together" but modifies that notion after she realizes, while watching the TV news report about "a dark-haired man with intense eyes and a badly inflected mouth," that Graves is the leper sex killer on top of everything else. "You're all I have left, Nancy," he says, adding, "I love you," but she runs off, needing time to think. After he encounters an infected couple down an alley, Graves flees into the night. Later he looks at his own reflection in a window, and in that merciful mirror he sees a smooth-skinned visage untouched by disease. "Nancy," he whispers. The next day he is running around town calling out her name. He finds her back at his place, sickened—scabby contusions on her chest and in her armpit as well as on her face—and he says her name once more after she dies. Then he hears the sirens outside (the story has looped back to its start) and grimly declares, "Now it begins."

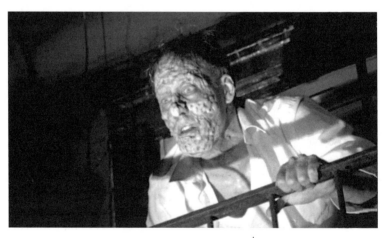

"Horror": futile protest (*Poison*).

Graves breaks down and weeps in a canted shot of his untidy living room: fluid, whether blood or infectious discharge, drips on his outstretched hands. He is distraught then angry, trashing the place, the camera spinning around. "Horror" ends with Graves's suicide, preceded by a speech to the gawping onlookers below. "Well, I'll tell you something. Every one of you down there is exactly the same, only you'll never know it . . . 'cause you'll never know what pride is, 'cause pride is the only thing that lets you stand up to misery—and not this kind of misery"—he gestures to his grotesque disfigurement—"but the kind of misery the whole stinking world is made of!" He jumps from the top of the fire-escape stairway, the camera twirling around before the viewpoint plummets (and plummets again) to the street below, members of the crowd screaming. When Graves opens his eyes for the last time, lying in a hospital bed, he sees in a delirious flash an old man with the buzzing wings of an angel—a final resurgence of *Poison*'s playfulness, though it counts for little compared to the way "Horror" has turned out. As Haynes says during the commentary: "Stuff that was ironic and tongue-in-cheek in the 'Horror' section—looking back on it, it's actually so sad, you know, it's hard even to laugh at it, given the whole AIDS epidemic . . . which of course it was always drawing on."

Poison explores three different scenarios of rebellion. In each storyline, society turns against characters, and normal belonging becomes impossible. Graves's ostracism is hard to bear in a particular way because he starts out an insider with a professional network. Unfairly disgraced, he skulks criminally and desperately in the shadows, and whenever he emerges he is despised for his disfigurement. His infectious symptoms cannot be hidden, and nor can he. The only mode of defiance left to him in his grief and furious terror is uselessly vengeful confrontation and the feeble demand that somehow the onlookers recognize their own servility. All he can do is spit back in the maw of the rather contented mob—whose readiness for this spectacle of sacrifice is a horror he now understands very well—and then throw his sick body down on them. There is no way out for Graves. His condemnation is as ineffective as flinging a grass snake into a pit full of vipers. Eloquent and truthful his denunciation may be, but it is just a drop of venom in a poisonous social sea. In counterattacking in this way, all Graves can do is set the timing of his demise. "Horror" thus represents the politics of futile protest, even though it is proud, and that is not nothing.

Punked

Slow, screechy fiddle playing accompanies the opening of "Homo," which is also the film's title sequence. A young hand explores the objects in a dim bedroom: a bird figurine, pearl necklace, silk scarf, tarot cards, a huge entomological book, and more. It is the late 1910s. The furtive rummaging is interrupted by a middle-aged foster couple's outrage. The title *Poison* appears onscreen at this point, suggesting the social nature of the toxin. It is the beginning of a boy's own story of exclusion: the rest of the story splits its time between teenage years spent at Baton Boys' Reformatory and adulthood in Fontenal Prison, which John Broom (Scott Renderer) enters at age thirty. Continuing Haynes's spoofing of medical categories, the admitting guard asks Broom about his "sexual behavior" ("the state obliges us" to ask, the jailer explains) and writes "Homo-sexual" where the form asks for "Previous Misdemeanors, Felonies, Mental Disturbances." Broom is disdainful of the process: "In submitting to prison life, embracing it, I could reject the world that had rejected me." Flashbacks to Baton make it seem like a bucolic gay refuge: peach-colored roses and iridescent lilies, ruined walls draped in wildflowers and ivy. Adolescent Broom (Tony Pemberton), wearing a lace veil, is betrothed there: "Harold Van Roven and John Broom do hereby pledge to one another in the eyes of their comrades and fellows in misery their loyalty and faith to one another's body and soul."

At Fontenal, Broom meets Jack Bolton, another Baton alumnus, played by James Lyons—who was the director's lover and collaborator for much of the 1990s, editing Haynes's films through *Far from Heaven* before his early death in 2007. The scenes in Fontenal rework Jean Genet's 1950 short *Un Chant d'amour*, an aching cinematic poem about sexual yearning famous for shots like the one of a prisoner blowing smoke through a hole in his cell wall, which is inhaled by the man next door. The fact that this source is silent adds to its sense of dreamlike remoteness: there is no room in it for the almost parodically macho sexual banter that occurs in Haynes's Fontenal, as when the top-dog prisoner, Rass (John R. Lombardi), goads a younger man with the words: "You swallow it by the mouthful, don't you birdie? Jism by the jug, right? You want it real bad, don't ya, punk? Don't ya, slug? . . . You want me to shoot it up yer hole, is that it, huh?" Fassbinder's *Querelle* (1982) much more convincingly adapts the toughness of Genet.

Institutionalized and imprisoned for much of his early life before everything was turned around by literary fame under the initial patronage of Jean-Paul Sartre, Genet never stopped attacking mainstream society, spurning the world that condemned him. In later life he was in the habit of rounding on television interviewers, and it is exhilarating to see the old man challenge his questioners. A notable example is when Genet took part in the BBC arts-documentary strand *Arena* in 1985 (available on YouTube). Rolling a cigarette, he starts up slowly and quietly: "I had a dream last night. I dreamed that the technicians of this little film revolted." In his dream, the crew decides to oust him from the interviewee's spot. Genet teases, exploring the reaction of the people in front of him, off-camera. He banters for a while before the interviewer says to him, with insipid astuteness: "But does it interest you to break the order of things? Since you were dreaming about it, do you want to break the order in this room?" Genet pounces: "To break the order? Of course. It seems too rigid. I'm all on my own here, and in front of me are one, two, three, four, five, six people. Of course I want to break the order. . . . I told you yesterday that you were behaving like policemen, and you're carrying on like that now, this morning. I told you yesterday, and you've already forgotten because you're continuing to interrogate me exactly like the thief I was thirty years ago, being interrogated by the police—by a squad of police. And I am alone on this little chair, being questioned by lots of people. There is the norm on one side where you are: one, two, three, four, five, six, seven, and elsewhere the editors of the film and the BBC, and then there is the margin where I am, where I am marginalized. If I am afraid to join the norm, then so be it. And if I am getting annoyed, it's because I am even now joining the norm. I'm going into English homes, and of course I'm not pleased. But I'm not annoyed with you for being part of the norm. I'm annoyed with myself for accepting to come here, and I'm really not pleased about that." Genet is right about the function played by the crew and about the institutional status of the British public broadcaster (an example of what Louis Althusser called an Ideological State Apparatus, if ever there was one); he is right to upset the equilibrium and challenge the format; and he is right too that he should not be there if he really wants to break that small piece of the order. The problem is that as long as he is there, he is in charge of the little drama in which he so grippingly role-plays subordination. And before the clip cuts out, with mild mischievousness he resets the game: "Well, ask me some questions, since the system requires that I'm the one that gets questioned."

In his rich, dense fiction, too, the French writer celebrated rejection and, in particular, the act of betrayal together with impersonal sex and other transgressions that go so far as to be called evil (and advocated nonetheless). This tendency was valorized by Bersani in *Homos,* with emphasis on a passage in *Funeral Rites* in which a French collaborator and a Nazi soldier have sex on a rooftop: "They were projecting the frightful ray of their love to infinity. . . . Erik and Riton were not loving one in the other, they were escaping from themselves over the world, in full view of the world, in a gesture of victory." Bersani reads this scene in a way that develops the Foucauldian analysis of sex's "deployment" as a form of social control: "Our culture tells us to think of sex as the ultimate privacy, as that intimate knowledge of the other on which the familial cell is built. Enjoy the rapture that will never be made public, that will also (though this is not said) keep you safely, docilely out of the public realm, that will make you content to allow others to make history while you perfect the oval of a merely copulative or familial intimacy. The sodomist, the public enemy, the traitor, the murderer (Erik and Riton answer to all these titles) are ideally unsuited for such intimacies (from the heterosexual family to the victorious Allies entering Paris), they are reduced, or elevated, to a kind of objectless or generalized ejaculation, a fucking of the world rather than each other" (165–66). Up on that Parisian roof, gay sex becomes a kind of tidal wave washing the two men psychically away so that they dissolve into the night.

Yet Haynes in *Poison* does not play up the all-transgressing loss of identity. In fact, it is precisely this side of Genet that he not only downplays but actually replaces with something far gentler, entirely out of keeping with his source's own emphasis. Speaking to Wyatt, Haynes explained that Genet "was deeply interested in what was particularly transgressive, and *only* what was transgressive, about homosexuality— and what was erotic about it as well. That went along with the under-ground, disturbing, dark, and at times intense betrayal of lovers and trusted people that is hard for a lot of people, including myself, to deal with" (7). He adds during the DVD commentary: "I never felt comfortable giving you Genet, giving you that transgression, that outsider experience, and so it had to sort of be filtered through dominant social points of view—to see how the outsider disrupts the mainstream world." And in a 2011 Sundance onstage discussion to mark the twentieth anniversary of *Poison* winning the Grand Jury Prize, included on the Zeitgeist anniversary DVD, he said: "I stepped in and I did my own interpretation and my own Americanization of ideas and perspectives that I gleaned from [Genet's] work." Nowhere is this more striking than in the scene in which Broom timidly undoes Bolton's fly (meeting no resistance) one night in a shared cell. "I love this scene," says Haynes during the commentary, "because I think it's just something that everyone's experienced in some way or other: sleeping beside someone you desire when you're in camp or whatever, and feeling all that tension and excitement." An American summer camp is far away from the violent and unethical universe of Genet's novels—just as this nighttime groping has little in common with the rooftop sex in *Funeral Rites*—but it has to be said that "Homo" is weakest when it adopts a tone of perverse machismo ("You want it real bad, don't ya, punk?"), and there is no attempt in this section of the film to represent the world-fucking that Bersani regarded as the most transgressive aspect of Genet's work. That comes instead in "Hero."

The encounter on the prison floor leads Bolton to say halfheartedly later, "You're my man" (Haynes wryly comments: "I guess it's hard to believe him"), and their intimacy almost immediately is jeopardized: "Bolton's friendship with Rass and the others filled me with jealousy that instigated a transformation. I felt myself growing mean, icy, stiff, gleaming like a sword blade." Broom turns cold with Bolton, and they fight. The Baton flashbacks conclude with the teenaged Bolton being punished ritualistically, furtively watched by Broom. Bolton (Andrew Harpending) stands in front of a wall, ordered to open his mouth while other inmates spit into it, both the fluid and the abjection linking "Homo" to "Horror." The spitting scene derives from *Funeral Rites,* and during the commentary Haynes says of his version: "This scene feels as violent as anything that Quentin Tarantino comes up with . . . the most disturbing thing for people is how ecstatic it is." The camera tilts up as the spitting continues, the bullies seeming to be able to float in the air as rose petals cascade down, and it rises and tilts down over Bolton, whose expression is an ambiguous mixture of humiliation and pleasure.

In an unpublished essay about Genet and Haynes's *Safe,* "Illegitimacy," Bersani identifies the imitative collusion and entrapment that are part of Genet's reject-the-world-that-rejected-me insubordination: "The escape from a judging world in the form of a total, willed immersion in it is at the extreme limit of subversive parody. Genet's demiurgic power would be to reinvent a world already given to him; his self-fashioning, however rebellious in intention, is no less a tautology." It is not, in short, an escape at all. Languorous intensity makes the spitting scene as much initiation ceremony as degradation.

Fontenal and Baton are strangely lawless areas. Guards are seen, but rarely, and so both institutions seem like quarantined areas as much as penitentiaries. They are places to fester not suffer, and it is the absence of misery that complicates the defiance shown in "Homo." As young Bolton is spat upon, his pacified expression conveys the distinct impression that he is beginning to like being cornered and insulted. To Graves's futile confrontation is added a more devious masochistic rebellion that subverts social cruelty by perverting and enjoying it. But to enjoy is not to oppose: masochistic defiance is a con trick that depends on the brutality it defrauds. There is no escape, and "Homo" ends with defeat: "Three days later, Rass took Bolton with him on an attempted escape from Fontenal. Rass made it as far as Orleans. Bolton was shot by a prison guard."

"Homo": erotic education (*Poison*).

Line of Flight

An earnest, fake-documentary female voice sets the scene for "Hero": "On June 3, 1985, at approximately 5:58 A.M., Richard Beacon, a seven-year-old Long Island boy, shot and killed his father in a heated family argument. Felicia Beacon, the boy's mother, astonishingly claims she then saw her son take off in flight from the patio balcony. What really happened the night of June 3? Who was Richie Beacon, and where is he now?" As the voiceover ends, the camera zeroes in on the face of Richie in a grainy family photo. At such proximity, underneath his baseball cap and in front of a low sun behind the picket fence, his face is just a mess of shadows with a clown's mouth, its ghostliness accentuated by the raster pattern.

The ensuing spoof of a prurient documentary gathers together churlish local gossips, school friends, and others to probe the mystery of murderous Richie's disappearance. But, in keeping with that death's-head photo, the departed object of this investigation remains strangely elusive in the tangle of competing, often spiteful recollections, and the problem is compounded by the rapturous opinion that Felicia (Edith Meeks) holds about her lost son: "I mean I punished him, his father hit him just like any kid, but I definitely didn't realize . . . that he was a gift from God." This is not how others describe him. A teacher at Park Street Elementary observes that "what was really strange was the amount of animosity he would induce in the other children, out of nowhere," and his fellow pupil Sean White (Ian Nemser) corroborates her account: "Some people felt sorry for him, but most of them wanted to hit him and stuff." Richie spent a lot of time in the office of the school nurse, Hazel Ramprecht (Marina Lutz), but as she tells it, he tended to be provocative. When he called her "fatso" one time, she admits: "I could have hurt him or something—I, I just, I think he was evil." The gym instructor remembers discovering Richie being roughly spanked by a slightly older boy, Gregory Lazar (Buck Smith), but Gregory tells it slightly differently: "He made me."

His mother's idea of Richie's innocence grows more and more tenuous. A doctor from the Cloyfield Medical Center discloses that "I found an infectious discharge—it was genitally secreted, a sharp yellow color," and Gregory goes into more detail about Richie's desire to role-play a son being beaten by his father plus his persistent demands that would eventually lead Gregory to "totally spank him just to make him shut up." Felicia starts to lose her composure as she relates the family context for Richie's disappearance. She and her husband, Fred, often fought; she was busy, and the boy "kept getting hurt." One night Fred tore up a flower bed, having previously fired the family gardener, José. Felicia's account becomes explicitly religious again: "I know that I was wrong, but my child was watching over me. My child was an angel of judgment, and I sinned against the Lord." Felicia confesses that, to her shame, Richie had walked in on her tryst with the family gardener (anticipating the more chaste scenario in *Far from Heaven*).

At last, fifteen minutes before *Poison*'s finale, after nothing but the backlit photo and anecdotes, Richie appears in frame. There is a piercing whistle on the sound track as he opens the door to witness (in a Super 8 shot-within-the-shot) his mother and José hastily covering themselves. Felicia's voiceover proceeds as there is a fast zoom-in to her face within the inserted shot before a cut to her onscreen interview: "When I saw his face it reminded me of this time, years before, when Fred was spanking Richie and I was watching and I swear he looked at me with the exact same expression. It was like some oath in some other language. His face was so weird. It made me feel ashamed." As this fanciful parent finishes the odd description of her son's facial oath, which has to be imagined for the reason that he is turned away, there is another mixed-shot image; Richie in a red shirt is lying on his front and again looking at his mother as if she were the TV, only this time his father is also there, spanking him. Felicia is on the right; Richie's body stretches from the center to the screen's left edge. All that can be seen of angry Fred is his hand and part of his forearm, which rise and fall as the punishment is administered.

There is a motif in Haynes's films that I call the out-of-line family. The recurring image is of two adults and a child, two of them looking one way, the third facing back in the opposite direction, though in this instance in *Poison*, one adult is only what a psychoanalyst might term a part object, not much more than a hand. The motif is somewhat cryptic because it does not depict a family that has been cut apart: maybe damaged bonds of intimacy will heal rather than breaking for good. These related shots focus the question of whether Haynes's films repudiate the family or are merely ambivalent toward it.

"Hero": the getaway (*Poison*).

Is *Poison*'s spanking scene erotic? Is this the rehearsal room for Richie's game with Gregory—the vestibule of Richie's sexuality? Haynes's spanking scenes, beginning with *Superstar,* self-consciously refer to psychoanalytic ideas about masochism, most directly in the reference in Haynes's next film, *Dottie Gets Spanked* (1993), to the 1919 essay "'A Child Is Being Beaten' (A Contribution to the Origin of Sexual Perversions)," in which Freud investigated the "beating-phantasies" of children and claimed to discover in them a yearning for parental love so insistent that sibling rivalry plays havoc with it. Freud described the simplest form of this incipient masochism as the dream of a sibling being punished: "One soon learns that being beaten, even if it does not hurt very much, signifies a deprivation of love and a humiliation. And many children who believed themselves securely enthroned in the unshakeable affection of their parents have by a single blow been cast down from all the heavens of their imaginary omnipotence. The idea of the father beating this hateful child is therefore an agreeable one, quite apart from whether he has actually been seen doing so. It means: 'My father does not love the child, *he loves only me*'" (172).

This theory has been debated a great deal, and even skeptics have continued to treat it as a family matter. Gilles Deleuze, a subsequent relentless opponent of what he and Félix Guattari called in *Anti-Oedipus* the "daddy-mommy-me" formula of psychoanalysis, objected to Freud in

"Coldness and Cruelty" but accepted his dramatis personae: "Masochism proceeds by a twofold disavowal, a positive, idealizing disavowal of the mother (who is identified with the law) and an invalidating disavowal of the father (who is expelled from the symbolic order)" (68). For all the permutations and divagations, there stand—or lie—father, mother, child. Eve Kosofsky Sedgwick recalled in "A Poem Is Being Written" her own experience of being spanked at home as "a small temporary visible and glamorizing theater around the immobilized and involuntarily displayed lower body of a child" (114). She then complicated this vignette of closeup reminiscence by stepping back from it and further populating it: "I see now—this is in Freud, too—that part of the effect of this concentration of framing is to eject from the *tableau* or table itself, along with every figure but the figure of part of the child, the entire visible mechanism of the gaze to which the child is exposed, the graphic multicharacter drama of infliction and onlooking, the visibly rendered plural possibilities of sadism, voyeurism, horror, Schadenfreude, disgust, or even compassion" (115). Maybe, but the scene is envisaged at the same time as it is enlarged to reveal these other witnesses—who are probably cruel, possibly compassionate, and in any case gathered there, a throng peering at the spectacle (that the writer in turn observes with all-seeing privilege). There seems to be no getting away from a bustling theater of family power.

But what if the child being spanked hardly even notices, and cares—let alone desires—still less? What if a spanking scene were not to entail all this family psychic rigmarole, were not a martyrology or theater of cruelty with who knows how many observed onlookers, but were instead an undoing of family, desire, meaning, representation? Perhaps all sexuality is masochistic to the extent that it reshapes and re-creates family ties (which would make heterosexuality a more tragic sexuality than homosexuality), and the alternative, if it could even still be called sexuality, is the ability to get out of family altogether, to break the family line in an act of queer antisocial destruction.

The complex image of Richie being spanked by his partly seen father does not need to be interpreted as a diagram of desire, even subversive desire. It can be looked at as something more minimal, less intricately interrelated to witnessed family power-playing. Richie seems oblivious to his father's punishment. His Sphinx-like expression transfixes his mother. Does she see the power of true negation in the boy's disdain? Richie's body is turned in powerful contempt away from Fred's useless violence, which neither intimidates the boy nor arouses him. Richie contests his father's authority and wins because his indifference is absolute. The boy even captures the father fragment. Looked at in a certain way, Fred's flapping arm appears like a part of his son's body—like a wing grown by Richie to lift him away from home.

Felicia remembers Richie's disconcerting expression when she sees it again before Richie kills Fred. The boy watches for a while as his mother is attacked—"You fucked him in my bed, huh," Fred growls, starting to throttle her. Felicia continues to narrate the dimly lit scene: "I remember him coming at me around the throat and me trying to hold his arms down, but he was like steel and I just thought, this is it. And then all of a sudden I hear this explosion. It was like a bomb and then another and then Fred just collapses on top of me. I look up, and Richie's standing there with the gun. I think he looked at me and then sort of took off toward the window. I was pulling Fred off of me when I saw him standing on the ledge and I screamed—I thought he was gonna jump. And then all of a sudden he did. He just jumped off the ledge and went up, like a wind or something had come and taken him because he was so light, but it wasn't the wind, he just took off. It was so weird when I ran and watched him go up. He just flew up. And I called to him and he sort of tilted my way before he kind of rolled out of sight. My little boy."

Members of the crew on the roof with extension poles achieved the swooping aerial shot that concludes *Poison*. As Haynes points out during the commentary, the setup can briefly be glimpsed reflected in the window out of which Felicia looks up toward her son who has taken flight. She is the only figure visible in the frame after Fred dies. The vantage point is high outside the bedroom window. The subjective camera backs away and then swings around so that a green blur of trees tilts past, and when that has gone there is total minimization—just the bright, blank whiteness of the sky.

Richie is not just a hero; he is a queer superhero. Unless the finale of *Poison* is interpreted psychoanalytically as a martyrdom fantasy, the boy's superpowers obviously include flight. But there is also what might be called Richie's homo-secrecy. Even in the family photo he seems in the process of vanishing. He confounds social containment: throughout "Hero" he runs rings around his neighbors, teachers, and parents, who compulsively spin conflicting stories that do no more than perpetuate his enigma. Richie is lacunary; he slips out of every snare set for him; he can hardly be found. Punishment strengthens him, and his calm contempt is lethal. The three-person family line is broken by an act born of Richie's indomitable apathy. He kills his father, leaves his mother to her caprices, and then escapes even the capture of representation in an image. Secretive, fugitive, radically disruptive, remorseless, he is the most transgressive character in Haynes's cinema. Neither dead nor imprisoned, Richie utterly surpasses Graves and Broom in the battle with society because when he soars away at the end of *Poison*, the whole of the visible world has been beaten.

Dottie Gets Spanked

Houses of Correction

In Fassbinder's *Fontane Effi Briest* (1974), a woman is disgraced when her long-finished affair with a soldier is discovered by chance. She sickens and is only accepted back into her parents' house after a debate between them in which her mother (Lilo Pempeit) argues from the position of propriety, irrespective of the welfare of Effi (Hanna Schygulla): "We're not just here to be kind and understanding towards things that are against laws and commandments and that society condemns, and rightly condemns at present." Her orthodox sentiment echoes something even more cynical stated earlier by a friend of Effi's husband: "The world is as it is. Things don't work out as we want them to, but as others want." During an interview collected in *The Anarchy of the Imagination*, Hella Schlumberger asked Fassbinder: "Isn't there any positive realm for you?" And he replied: "Not for me. It seems to me the society I live in is shaped not by happiness and freedom but rather by oppression, fear, and guilt. In my opinion, what we're taught to experience as happiness is a pretext that a society shaped by various forms of compulsion offers the individual" (21). The German director's films mainly show life at its most punishing, and sometimes—as in *The Merchant of Four Seasons* (1971) and *Fox and His Friends* (1975)—they end with a corpse on the ground. Family life comes apart at the seams to reveal the ugly mechanisms of social cruelty inside it. Glimpses of a tolerable world, let alone a better one, are few. In a video interview on the Arrow Films DVD of *Fear Eats the Soul,* Haynes acknowledged the inspiration of Fassbinder's work and the theme, also developed by Sirk, of "people trapped in houses and social morality." And, Haynes added, "that's where we all intersect as subjects in a corrupt society, under the auspices of moral, domestic culture." There is a heart of darkness in the family home.

The institutions of a subtly oppressive society need to cloak power and if possible convince those who submit that it involves no hardship. In "Freud and Lacan," Althusser described childhood as secret conscription: "The only war without memoirs or memorials, the war humanity pretends it has never declared, the war it always thinks it has won in advance, simply because humanity is nothing but surviving this war, living and bearing children as culture in human culture: a war which is continually declared in each of its sons, who, projected, deformed, and rejected, are required, each by himself in solitude and against death, to take the long forced march which makes mummiferous larvae into human children" (190). The veiling matters very much, the war's concealment of itself, even its pretended resemblance to something gentle, happy, permissive. As Foucault put it in *The History of Sexuality,* "[P]ower is tolerable only on condition that it mask a substantial part of itself. . . . Its success is proportional to its ability to hide its own mechanisms. Would power be acceptable if it were entirely cynical? For it, secrecy is not in the nature of an abuse; it is indispensable to its operation. Not only because power imposes secrecy on those whom it dominates, but because it is just as indispensable to the latter: would they accept it if they did not see it as a mere limit placed on their desire, leaving a measure of freedom—however slight—intact?" (86). An iron hand likes a velvet glove, and the thirty-minute TV film *Dottie Gets Spanked* deals with a most ordinary form of the kind of smart, soft power that offers consolation prizes as well as discipline and punishment.

A Child Is Not Being Beaten

Dottie Gets Spanked spoofs the title of Freud's masochism essay in a silent-film-style intertitle that reads: "A child is being beaten on its naked bottom." But there is in fact no such nakedness onscreen. Every bottom seen is clothed at least by underpants, and an even more significant aspect of *Dottie Gets Spanked* is that no one is really spanked in it. Instead there is a series of not-quite-spankings that together suggest the insidiousness of domestic coercion.

Steven Gale, called Stevie (J. Evan Bonifant), likes to sit right in front of the TV, his sketchpad on his knees, to watch *The Dottie Show,* Haynes's fiction equivalent of *I Love Lucy.* When a neighbor (Harriet Harris) visits his mother Lorraine (Barbara Garrick) and mentions in his hearing that she has "never seen a child get so many spankings" as her daughter Sharon, Stevie finds his attention divided between the object of his devoted fandom and the obscurely alluring tale of the type of domestic castigation his parents refrain from. As Lorraine explains to her friend, "We just don't believe in hitting, Evan and I." Although the two mothers may disagree on the method, it becomes clear that they share a belief that parents need to keep children in line. The way these two mothers volubly differ on the topic of spanking increases the domestic threat level for Stevie. Irrespective of the opinion on family bullying, the conversation itself creates a manipulative environment that would be more disturbing if it did not seem so normal.

Stevie fills in a magazine prize coupon in an attempt to win a visit to the set of *The Dottie Show.* Evan (Robert Pall) disapproves and in frustration sends the boy to bed. That night, Stevie dreams vividly: he sits on a castle-topped throne wearing a crown that is nearly as high as he is and with imperious intolerance rejects out of hand an armor-clad Dottie's plea that he come to watch her show. Tinkling chimes shift the dream scene to a walled courtyard (in the style of de Chirico) in which a man is spanking a boy with increasing vigor. The dense montage sequence also includes a brief image of Sharon (Ashley Chapman), so this is the dreamer's elaboration of what Sharon's mother said—this is the way the domestic power talk got through to Stevie. If the frantic, spectacular nature of the dream suggests rebellious glee, fascination, and desire, its jittery creativity comes out of alarm and disorientation, which are apt responses to the menace of the mothers' chitchat. This dream of punishment is not quite a spanking, though, precisely because it is a dream.

When Stevie wakes up early the next morning, the sound of his parents talking drifts through the wall. "It's one night a week," says Lorraine. "It's one night a week, but he spends the other six days waiting for the show, drawing pictures," Evan replies. Stevie's six-year-old face is powerlessly inexpressive as he lies in the bluish dawn light having to hear this domestic disciplinary tribunal in whispers. Thus *Dottie Gets Spanked* presents Stevie's discovery of two contrasting kinds of loneliness—the rambunctious but uneasy dream, the accidental isolated eavesdropping—that are inevitable side-effects of his failure to conform to the family line.

At school, other boys mock him for his smart bowling shoes and red earmuffs while the *Dottie*-mad girls unkindly find his shared interest hilarious. Sharon's younger sibling rushes up to him after school to declare with delight: "My sister says you're a feminino!" Again there is intimidating suburban chatter that does not overdo aggression. At home, an excited Lorraine tells Stevie that he has won the contest. Together they look through his Dottie sketchbooks in preparation for the trip to the studio in New York. On that special morning, Evan sits Stevie down in the bathroom and combs his son's hair. This grooming scene epitomizes a carefully determined mode of parental control just as Evan's cold look of disapproval does whenever he sees his son doing something he does not like.

Stevie, wearing a bow tie and double-breasted blue-green sports jacket, is the only boy among the four prize winners at NBS Studios. Another fantasy is triggered by a scene being filmed in which Dottie (Julie Halston) and then her stand-in are spanked by her fictional spouse. The sequence that follows plays a lighter variation on the breakdown in *Superstar.* Again, clean-cut TV images are distorted—the fake sitcom scene, Dottie recostumed in a bright red evening dress and pearls in Stevie's mind's eye, is refilmed in rasterized closeup—to indicate a moment of psychic upheaval.

There is a trio of not-quite-spankings in the studio scene. What happens in front of the TV cameras is staged comedy performed farcically by adults. Stevie processes it, first as subject matter for his second onscreen dream, and then for another lurid crayon drawing: these are his records of a simulation, twice removed from a spanking that would be worthy of the name. When his father sees Stevie instinctively covering it up, Evan gets the picture out from under his hands anyway. At least the three girls who had previously spurned Stevie gather around him in the playground later, eager to hear his account of the day. But before he can begin he is distracted by the sound of an angry parent—"What the hell did you just say to me?!"—lashing out at his son near the gate, slapping the boy hard on the back. This is the closest *Dottie Gets Spanked* comes to showing spanking pure and simple, but without the context of domestic ritual this blow is better described as socially permitted petty battery.

The decision of the dawn tribunal finally comes into the open when his parents interrupt Stevie's Dottie-viewing. Evan is standing; Lorraine is perched on the edge of the sofa; in the background Stevie, with his sketchpad on his knees, looks back at them with a mixture of anxiety and petulance. It is the next instance of the motif of the out-of-line family,

The out-of-line family (*Dottie Gets Spanked*).

the power relations accentuated by the elevated camera position, the downward angle of the shot emphasizing that Stevie is hopelessly over-matched. "What if tonight you try maybe watching something Daddy likes watching, something that the two of you could watch together?" says Lorraine. Dottie is groaning on the TV as Stevie storms out of the room with futile disobedience, cueing the return in the boy's final fantasy of the comic monarch stamping a black-booted foot and reprimanding Dottie in no uncertain terms: "Never! It is forbidden in this country! Never!" Stevie is dreaming uneasily in bed again. Stern, accusatory, jeering faces reminiscent of "Horror" loom in the boy's private film. A cage drops over the once-mighty sovereign, and a medieval apparatchik pronounces: "Steven Gale, you are 100 percent guilty, and so you must submit to the highest sentence in the land!" His sentence is to find "the strongest man in the kingdom," who in fact finds Stevie, plucking the boy out of his confinement and placing him over his knee. When Richie looks over his shoulder, a mustachioed Dottie has materialized in the strongman's place. A breakneck montage of all the previous castigation scenes ensues that also includes a repeated color image of Stevie grinning exultantly. He seems to have mounted an unseen animal—the clip-clop of horse hooves can be heard on the sound track—and his free hand is raised at first in a spanking-type gesture. His expression is jubilant. This is a moment of masochistic initiation by means of which Stevie learns—in the defeated manner of "Homo"—to take surreptitious pleasure (Foucault's paltry "measure of freedom") in his own humiliation and indoctrination, but it is more delirious bronco-riding than spanking.

When Stevie wakes up, he must reckon on another wintry morning with a concerted campaign against the deviance of his Dottie delight. He is six and three-quarters, without superpowers. He cannot effectively resist. So he folds up the colorful drawing of Dottie bent over her husband's knee, wraps it in aluminum foil, and buries it in a flowerbed in the dark before the dawn. He pats down the earth, covering this little war memorial of misfit desire. Haynes says during the commentary that Stevie "sort of spanks it into the future," but this is not a spanking so much as a necessary capitulation to the sort of quiet and intimate power that knows how much can be accomplished in a bathroom barbershop.

Safe

Outpatients

Take two images of psychic blankness. First, Edward Hopper's 1952 painting *Morning Sun,* which Haynes spoke about in discussion with Dyer in 2004. A woman is sitting on a bed in a spartan room. She is in profile, and her visible right eye is like a black bead. Such bright light is pouring through the window, it is as if an atomic bomb were exploding outside that had somehow already incinerated her eyes. As Haynes describes the painting, "There's darks in it, but there's nothing as black as her eyes, and her eyes aren't detailed. It's almost like a bullet hole, it's a void. There's nothing in her gaze." Then, in Haynes's one rock video, for Sonic Youth's suggestively entitled 1990 track "Disappearer," a traveling shot taken from a car briefly frames a black-clad young man looking at the camera as he stands alone on the nighttime street. His face is expressionless, yet he seems serene rather than vague. Since there is a bandage on his head, he could be an escapee from a psychiatric ward where he has been lobotomized. Or he could be a zombie, an alien, even an angel. His fleeting mysteriousness, though, suggests another possibility: a blankness outside social belonging and personal identity. The man could be a homo, in Bersani's use of the word: beings that "renounce self-ownership and agree to the loss of boundaries" (*Homos* 128).

Carol White in *Safe* (or *[SAFE]*, as the title card has it) is the wife of an executive who spends her days in the San Fernando Valley, California, refurbishing her affluent gated home, lunching, taking aerobics classes. In some wide shots—speaking on the phone in a lounge room with egg-shaped floor lamps, standing by the pool in darkness—she seems like just another decorative domestic object: a figurine or piece of furniture. She is passive and placid, never angry or indignant. Though Carol would have reason to say something similar, it is impossible to imagine her speaking to her husband as Nora does in Henrik Ibsen's *The Doll's House*: "Our house has never been anything but a play-room. I have been your doll wife, just as at home I was Daddy's doll child. And the children in turn have been my dolls. I thought it was fun when you came and played with me, just as they thought it was fun when I went and played with them. That's been our marriage, Torvald" (80–81). Nevertheless, could it be that despite being (as Haynes put it to Dyer) "so far from the suggestion of desire"—or in fact because of this—she is a homo too?

If it is not mere hiding or abdicating, disappearing may be (as with Richie's homo-secrecy in *Poison*) a much more effective opposition to an imprisoning social apparatus than ostentatious defiance. (This is one implication of Herman Melville's much-debated story "Bartleby, the Scrivener," in which a clerk politely refuses, without giving any reason, to do as he is told: he creates a vortex in the discourse of obedient self-justification, and this discomfits his employer—it drives him half-crazy with perplexity—far more than any arguing could.) If disappearing is not in itself a counterattack, perhaps it is necessary preparation. Near the end of *Anti-Oedipus,* Deleuze and Guattari approvingly quote a passage from Maurice Blanchot's 1971 book *Friendship* (the original context is a discussion of Albert Camus's novel *The Fall*): "The world is poorly chosen to please. Courage consists, however, in agreeing to flee rather than live tranquilly and hypocritically in false refuges. Values, morals, homelands, religions, and these private certitudes that our vanity and our complacency bestow generously on us, have as many deceptive sojourns as the world arranges for those who think they are standing straight and at ease, among stable things." Camus's character of Clamence, according to Blanchot, labors under no such deception; he achieves "escape in advance of the escape" because he "is no longer able to stand living in the false pretenses of residence" (341).

"Oh God, what is this? Where am I? Right now?" When Carol confesses to her husband Greg (Xander Berkeley) that she feels inexplicably transported and lessened, she is in great distress. She is not sure of her identity or whether there is a place she belongs. All Greg can think of to say is, "We're in our house, Greg and Carol's house," and a cut to the couple's bedside wedding photo emphasizes the mismatch between their home and his "we," on the one hand, and her strange internal exile from them both, on the other hand. She is present but somehow not resident. This is evidently hard for her, but it is not exactly involuntary, and indeed the difficulty of thinking about Carol's incomplete—failed—disappearing act in *Safe* lies with a preconception that it would be better for her if she could just find herself again, feel at home, reconnect with her desires, get back to the safety of love and belonging.

Margaret Atwood's 1985 dystopian fiction *The Handmaid's Tale* is narrated by a fertility slave in an elite enclave. At one point, the narrator muses on her loneliness in captivity: "It's lack of love we die from. There's nobody here I can love, all the people I could love are dead or elsewhere. Who knows where they are or what their names are now? They might as well be nowhere, as I am for them. I too am a missing person" (113). But *Safe* suggests for a while that the loveless—or beyond-desire—condition of going missing might actually be better than the bonded, located, nameable alternative. Carol may not be a victim when she appears like an object or a fugitive wraith in what Blanchot called a false refuge.

Lost in the Kitchen

Safe's soundtrack record by Ed Tomney is separated into four acts—"The Symptoms," "Question of Illness," "Lost at Wrenwood," and "The Final Discovery." Tomney's score is eerie, otherworldy, sinister. Played by the composer using "keyboards, analog and digital synthesizers, prepared electric guitar and bass, various fabricated electro-acoustic instruments, guitar trees & other components from The Industrial Orchestra, analog tape composition," to quote the CD description, it is futuristic music for a time of emergency—for the plague years. The title theme is paradoxical because its rudimentary, slowly rising melody suggests danger more than safety; the title sequence's nighttime car journey through a prosperous suburban housing development has the mood, because of this ominous music, of a journey through a military compound or some sprawling science-fiction asylum complex.

It is 1987 in southern California. Behind the expensive electric gate is the home Carol shares with Greg and her stepson, Rory (Chauncey Leopardi). Carol's first words upon returning there, responding to Greg's "bless you" after she sneezes in the garage, are: "It's freezing in here." The family displays plenty of affection, but there is no mistaking the fact that during conjugal intercourse in the next scene, Carol is neither aroused nor even comfortable (though she makes no explicit objection). Filmed from above, this short scene is the first of several allusions to Chantal Akerman's feminist anti-epic *Jeanne Dielman, 23 Quai du Commerce, 1080 Bruxelles* (1975). In Akerman's penultimate scene, the part-time prostitute Jeanne (Delphine Seyrig) is, despite her customary affectlessness, brought to orgasm by her john, which prompts her to stab him to death with a pair of scissors. The inexpressive Carol never gets excited and commits no act of aggression, yet the recollection of Akerman's film implies a question: Does Carol live the same kind of alienated existence that drives Jeanne to murder? If so, does Carol enact a nonviolent form of resistance to the domestic torpor?

The next morning, Carol is pruning yellow roses in the front garden when Greg says goodbye blandly on his way to work. The first of many wide, objectifying shots shows the house's impressive façade, which dwarfs the two people. This repeated distancing technique reflects one starting point for *Safe*—Haynes's discomfort with a conversation that took place during a festive gathering at his parents' home attended by his uncle and his uncle's girlfriend Mary. He explained to Oren Moverman in "And All Is Well in Our World": "After dinner, we were all in the living room, and Mary all of a sudden turned to Barry and said, 'Barry, remember that bet we had on the plane? The bet about the faggot?' Everyone just kind of stopped doing what they were doing for a second, and I could just tell that this shiver ran down their spines. I tried to carry on normally, half overhearing them, and she went on, 'Me and Barry were sitting on the plane and there was a faggot sitting in between us. And we made a bet whether the faggot would move so we could sit next to each other. We asked him, and finally he did.' Later I was so angry at myself for not saying something. It hit such a personal note that I didn't know how to respond at that moment. So I felt angry and shocked by this, but at the same time I felt so intrigued by this woman. She just seemed so far away from me. She was someone really from another set of values or cultural assumptions. As opposed to wanting to kill her, I felt challenged by her, and challenged by my own inability to understand her. It made me imagine coming up with some narrative access to somebody as far away from me as that, somebody who I might have a really severe set of resistances to, prejudices against, dismissals of—intellectual or otherwise. I wanted to find her. I don't think this represents Carol White directly, but it was the beginning of a challenge to me in terms of how to find a character like that and bring her closer to me in film" (200).

Carol follows a leisurely routine. She goes to exercise class wearing Lycra (Madonna's "Lucky Star" is the accompaniment) and chats with other participants in the locker room afterwards: "You know, Carol, you do not *sweat*," observes one. She meets a friend whose brother has just died. Back at home, Carol speaks on the phone to someone she calls "mother" (maybe her mother-in-law, since there is something so orphaned about Carol) and then discovers that the wrong-colored sofa pair (black, not teal) has been delivered. She is assertive as she gets the company on the phone. Haynes's script plays up almost to the point of parody a sense of valley-wife vacuity at first (the way Carol refers oddly to the "coming-out part" of the sofa, the stilted Spanish she speaks to her maid), yet it is soon clear that this protagonist is uncanny more than comic. If Carol seems lacking, what is involved is not stupidity or just the banality of her wealthy milieu but rather some lack of responsiveness that characterizes her disjoined relations with her environment. When she childishly drinks a glass of milk the next day, house painters working in the kitchen behind her, the camera slowly moving toward her in a track-and-zoom shot, the "Carol's Milk" theme an electro echo chamber, she seems not enigmatic but profoundly simplified, just another vessel for the pale liquid. Carol lacks some thickness or density of personality—having only enough sociability to be consistently personable and kindly. There is a further link here to *Jeanne Dielman* (a scene in which Jeanne tests milk for sourness), but also to the opening of Stanley Kubrick's *A Clockwork Orange* (1971)—Haynes cites Kubrick as one of the main influences on the look of *Safe*—which features a long track-back from a quartet of milk-drinking thugs preparing to go on the rampage. As with the sex scene at the beginning, antisocial hostility hovers in the intertextual background to scenes of Carol's passivity.

In the 1960s through the 1970s, filmmakers engaged with feminism by dramatizing situations of discontent, suffering, or abuse in the home and in marriage. The spectrum of this exploration of shared premises can be seen in the contrast between two heartfelt statements made by characters to doctors. In *The Stepford Wives* (dir. Bryan Forbes, 1975), on the run from the community of husbands that is systematically replacing wives with androids, Joanna (Katharine Ross) confesses to a medic from whom she has sought refuge: "There will be somebody with my name, and she'll cook and clean like crazy, but she won't be *me* . . . she'll be like one of those robots in Disneyland." In a different vein, there is a melancholy disclosure by Bree (Jane Fonda) to her analyst in Alan J. Pakula's *Klute* (1971): "I don't really give a damn. What I would really like to do is be faceless and bodiless and be left alone." The one character fears a loss of her own identity; the other claims to desire effacement and disappearance.

Identity crisis is related to sexuality and its discontents in these films. In another acknowledged influence on *Safe*, *Red Desert* (dir. Michelangelo Antonioni, 1964), Giuliana (Monica Vitti), who has been institutionalized in the recent past after a suicide attempt, suffers nameless dread: "You can't imagine the fears I have," she says to Corrado (Richard Harris). At first she describes her time under medical supervision in the third person, reluctant to identify herself to Corrado. Under this disguise, she recounts: "The doctor told her, 'You should learn how to love. Love a person or a thing. Love your husband, your son, a job, even a dog.'" The task she is given is to reactivate her desire. In *A Woman under the Influence* (dir. John Cassavetes, 1974), Mabel (Gena Rowlands) is also institutionalized against her will, and when she comes back, docile, she disconcerts her gathered family by bringing its secret demand into the open (recall Foucault's critique of the "repressive hypothesis") and announcing her longing to be alone with her husband: "I wish you'd all go home—Nick and I want to go to bed together." These women-back-from-the-verge films associate sanity with a normally functioning desire. Troubled characters return to themselves when desire is replenished, and conversely, the condition of self-erasure is treated as a threat to health, family, and the order of things. This is especially vivid in *A Woman under the Influence* when Nick (Peter Falk) and his mother Margaret (Katherine Cassavetes) turn on Mabel after her erratic behavior exceeds their tolerance: "I don't know who you are!" he shouts. Margaret goes further: "He tells me stories of the talk, the small talk . . . the insecurities. . . . He says you give him nothing. You're empty inside."

Yet this emptiness could be a kind of liberation. This would explain why it is so infuriating, so threatening, like Richie's mischief and secrecy in "Hero." To stop being a person is to go missing from the world of social obligation in a refusal of the linked doctrines of family belonging and self-help. In his 1960 book *The Divided Self*, R. D. Laing included a case history he called "The Ghost of the Weed Garden" in which he described a female patient's schizophrenic distress: "She said the trouble was that she was not a real person; she was trying to become a person. There was no happiness in her life and she was trying to find happiness. She felt unreal and there was an invisible barrier between herself and others. She was empty and worthless" (178–79). What if trying to be a person could be what is wrong, not the invisible wall or the emptiness? In order for this to be conceivable, though, it is necessary to abandon what Bersani called "the sacrosanct value of selfhood" ("Is the Rectum a Grave?" 30) and think about antisocial modes of being utterly incompatible with family values and the disparate psychologies that reinforce them.

Shrinking

While she is driving, truck fumes cause Carol to start coughing, first gently and then as if she were being throttled. It is all she can do to bring the car to a halt in an underground lot. That night, she is still recovering from the attack: she dozes in a white satin dressing gown on the unwanted black sofa in front of the TV, which plays some sort of infomercial about "deep ecology." When she cannot sleep, she stands in the dark like a frail specter by the poolside gazebo, light reflected off the water dappling her silky white back, which is all that can be seen of her.

She zones out during a sexually explicit joke Greg's colleague makes at a restaurant later, causing Greg to send Carol to Dr. Hubbard (Steven Gilborn), who simply says, "I really don't see anything wrong with you, Carol," gives her some ointment and decongestant, and warns her off too much fruit or dairy. (Carol, unperturbed, speculates that she is stressed and admits that she is a "total milkaholic.") But something is definitely wrong. At the salon—more upbeat pop playing, this time Billy Ocean's "Get Outta My Dreams, Get into My Car"—where she impulsively decides to have a perm, she suddenly gets a nosebleed. Back home, she complains of a headache and "a touch of something" when she tells disgruntled Greg that she does not want to have sex with him. "I know it's not normal, but I can't help it," she adds, sitting on the edge of the bed in their affluent bedroom with its mirror-walled closet. In the next, brief scene—she presumably has not been able to sleep again—Carol is in the living room looking at a family photo. Is she losing access to her memories? Has she started to involuntarily shed the skin of the past? The next morning, she breaks her husband's embrace in order to vomit, and so she goes back to the doctor, this time with Greg in tow. The physician refers her to a psychiatrist.

Carol's sleeplessness continues, and she mooches by the roses in her nightgown. There is something both intriguing and illicit about Carol's wandering. She is filmed from behind by a moving camera, and there is a touch of *Vertigo* (dir. Alfred Hitchcock, 1958) in the way it shadows her. She could be a vampire in the making, or half-phantom, or she could be scouting the perimeter for the best escape route. Yet Carol cannot walk at night without drawing the attention of the security guards employed in this prosperous encampment. They shine a powerful flashlight at her, and she flinches in the beam before going back inside. Greg is awake and waiting. Looking down at her from the landing, he asks: "What are you doing, honey?" His vigilance makes the nocturnal house a security zone too; he does the patrol car's work on the inside. Carol answers the question as if she had just been explicitly rebuked: "I couldn't sleep: the air, the smell." Domestic safety is becoming uncomfortable for her.

After the next aerobic class, Carol's attention is caught by an orange flyer that reads: "Do you smell *FUMES*? Are you allergic to the 20th century? Do you have trouble breathing? Is your drinking water pure? Do you suffer from skin irritations? Are you always tired?" The interest she gives to this document contrasts with her bland, factual responses

Security light (*Safe*).

to the psychiatrist in the next scene. Not only does she have, it seems, nothing to divulge to him, she also asks: "Aren't you supposed to ask more questions?" With condescension, he responds: "Well, no. We really need to be hearing from you. What's going on in you?" But the problem must be that this oddly phrased final question presupposes a capacity in Carol that she may not have. Does she possess the depth of personality that would make sense of that "in"?

Do not trust a psychoanalyst: this warning emerges from a series of post-1968 supernatural films and radical theory from the same period. In *Invasion of the Body Snatchers* (dir. Philip Kaufman, 1978), *Rosemary's Baby* (dir. Roman Polanski, 1968), and *The Stepford Wives,* shrinks betray their patients to those who mean great harm. These movies corroborate the suspicious claim in Deleuze and Guattari's *Anti-Oedipus*: "As to those who refuse to be oedipalized in one form or another, at one end or the other in the treatment, the psychoanalyst is there to call the asylum or the police for help" (81). Suspicion of the profession was even more vividly stated by the playwright Antonin Artaud in a 1946 piece, "Van Gogh: The Man Suicided by Society": "Medicine is born of evil, if it is not born of disease, and it has even, on the contrary, provoked sickness out of whole cloth in order to give itself a reason for being; but psychiatry is born of the vulgar black earth of people who have wished to maintain the evil at the source of illness and who have thus rooted out of their own nothingness a kind of Swiss Guard, to sap the rebellious drive which is the origin of all geniuses" (144).

When Carol goes to the analyst, she does not cause obvious trouble, yet her blandness confounds this medic sitting in front of a pair of tapestries depicting a jungle and a monkey. The scene disarms authority in something like the manner of the spanking scene in "Hero." Does Carol make psychoanalysis impossible? She does not use the time to reflect on her predicament; however different the statements are in *The Stepford Wives* and *Klute,* both times the character is taking analysis seriously, talking through her existential dread, her crises of being and desire. Carol does nothing of the sort; nor does she protest, as Mabel understandably does in *A Woman under the Influence* when she sees that her husband has brought a doctor home with him: "No one here needs a doctor. . . . Nick, I get the idea there's some kind of a conspiracy going on here. I mean, you've been looking at me so quiet, like, and he's got something in that bag—he's going to imprison me with something in that bag." Instead of revealing herself to the analyst, Carol might be said to blind him, shimmering, dazzling, as if she were halfway to teleporting out of there. She is not exactly compliant, but she blocks the shrink by offering no topics for discussion, no symptoms of desire run amok, no interest even in thinking out loud. Her passivity outwits the institutional, biopolitical control-through-participation. It is the opposite of the scene in *A Woman under the Influence*: in *Safe,* the doctor is unsettled, not the patient. Faced with Carol's elusiveness, the doctor even starts to get a little resentful, demanding to know what is "in you," as if he were a customs official inspecting luggage.

At a friend's baby shower, Carol seems distracted. She sits with a child on her knee, watching a stroller being unwrapped, and starts, in the way the health-club notice described, to have trouble breathing. She wheezes terribly like she did in the parking lot, panicked and disturbed, almost suffocating. It is becoming impossible for Carol to reside in the world that is familiar to her. Suddenly, everyone around her has to keep watch for fear of what might happen. She is a disappearer, sick without diagnosis. According to Bersani in "Illegitimacy," referring to the garden scenes: "Carol makes no conscious political choices; she is, constitutively, a refusal to belong, to be named. Haynes even suggests . . . that, apart from the social and environmental oppressiveness that victimizes her, she is in the 'wrong' universe." If only Carol could have found a way out of the comfortable security zone during one of her walks. But instead she goes somewhere worse.

Retreat

Safe transitions to a new phase of the narrative, announced by an unexpected voiceover—a self-asserting device that starts to correct her almost-vanishing act—heard over a shot of more family photos (wedding day, graduation, relatives) that ends with her sitting up in bed writing the letter whose words are being spoken: "My name is Carol White, and I live in southern California. I saw your notice at the health club near my house and decided to write and tell you a little bit about myself. For some time now I have not been feeling up to par and was hoping your organization might be of some help. I'm originally from Texas, although I've lived in the L.A. area most of my life. I had asthma as a child, but it never really got in the way of school or recreation. I've always thought of myself as someone with a pretty normal upbringing and basically as a petty healthy person, but for the past several months that has all started to change. Suddenly I find myself feeling sick." It is at this point that she says to Greg that she is not even sure where she is.

Carol takes the path that opened up when she saw the notice at the health club. She attends a morning presentation about environmental illness and submits to a battery of allergy tests, her body becoming a temporarily tattooed medical chart in the clinic. The doctor conducting the tests comfortingly explains the process, but Carol suddenly suffers a reaction, "a biggie," the medic calls it: "We have palpitations and deep distress in conjunction with a racing pulse rate of 104. There's flushing and some wheezing, a little swelling in the mouth." She goes to another environmental-illness group, at which a woman for the first time says the name Wrenwood, referring to the desert recovery community Carol will soon unfortunately join. That there were other possible paths is suggested by the scene that follows: Carol joins a group of six other women (among them a character played by Edith Meeks—Felicia in *Poison*) outside the meeting venue. They converse supportively, more than one decrying the notion—predominant at Wrenwood—that environmental illness is psychosomatic. Carol is now committed to self-help: a plethora of tablet bottles appear on the table in front of her at home; she listens to a tape about chemical "load" and detoxifying; she makes up a bed in a safe room with aluminum foil stuck to the floor ("safe bodies need safe environments to live," says the woman on the tape); an oxygen tank on wheels accompanies her on shopping trips, and she wears a surgical mask. But the precautions—if that is what they indeed are—prove insufficient, and her worst breakdown occurs at the dry cleaners. She is rushed to the hospital. In an overhead shot, a bloody towel is crumpled on the stretcher next to her face.

Greg and Dr. Hubbard are frustrated by Carol's insistence that she is ill as a result of a disorder of the immune system that makes her hypersensitive to chemicals in the environment: the physician insists that no evidence corroborates this self-diagnosis. But Carol's mind is made up, and she departs Los Angeles for Wrenwood after it is mentioned again on the hospital TV: "Nestled in the foothills of Albuquerque, the

Wrenwood Center describes itself as a nonprofit communal settlement dedicated to the healing individual, offering the services of a combined health retreat and community center." Its founder, Peter Dunning, plugs the establishment, calling it "a kind of safe haven for troubled times."

She arrives at the desert outpost in a cab driven by James Lyons. But as the car approaches the gate, a woman frantically calls that it is "not allowed": "Go back," she cries, "you're contaminating this entire area!" This is a place where a world regarded as poisonous is kept as much as possible at bay. It is a makeshift settlement consisting of low, cheaply constructed huts as well as a circular brick building that houses workshop space, a chapel, and dining facilities. Overlooking the much humbler dwellings is a palatial house where Peter, a successful self-help writer and (it is explained to Carol) "chemically sensitive person with AIDS, so his perspective is incredibly vast," lives. Haynes debated whether such an incriminating shot should be included, but even if it had not been, the character of Peter would have been recognizable as to some degree a fraud and manipulator. He even seems to have his own trademark prayer: "We are one with the power that created us, we are safe, and all is well in our world." His address to a gathering of all the staff and residents is sheer quackery: "Welcome to Wrenwood. Alright. If you'd all close your eyes and pass your valuables to the front. No, no, come on! Not really. Okay, so we're feeling good, huh? We're feeling warmth? We can look into each other's eyes and actually see rejuvenation and personal transformation happening. Why? Because we've left the judgmental behind. Phew. And with it the shaming condition that kept us locked up in all the pain. But what I want to share with you tonight, what I want to give you tonight, is an image to reflect on, an image of a world outside as positive and as free as the world we've created here. Because when you look out on the world from a place of love and a place of forgiveness, what you are seeing outside is a reflection of what you feel within. Does that make sense? So: what do I see outside me? I see the growth of environmentalism, right? And holistic study. I see a decline in drugs and promiscuity. I see sensitivity training in the work-place! And the men's movement and multiculturalism! I see all these positive things outside in the world because what I am seeing is a global transformation identical to the transformation I revel at within!"

Birthday Flowers

There is something obviously seedy and hokey about Peter, who refuses to read the papers or watch TV for fear his immune system will "believe" any bad news. Just below the surface he seems mean and vain. In a group session, after an ambulance has taken a resident away, Peter speaks through what might as well be gritted teeth: "Let's throw away every negative, destructive thought we might have and look around ourselves with love. I tried to teach him this: to give up the rage." The frail old man's removal has become a pretext for this modern-day shaman's self-congratulation. Then, at an outdoor discussion, Peter becomes pious and hectoring when the bereaved Nell (Mary Carver) objects to the "I made myself sick" doctrine, refreshingly preferring to blame others: "I just wanted to get a gun and blow off the heads of everyone who got me like this." He tells her to remember her affirmations and "figure out how to love Nell a lot more—and even Nell's disease—and put that gun of yours away." The ideas voiced here refer to the work of the multi-million-selling guru Louise L. Hay, whose 1984 book *You Can Heal Your Life* claimed that "mental patterns . . . create dis-eases in the body" and speculated that the "probable cause" of AIDS is "[f]eeling defenseless and hopeless. Nobody cares. A strong belief in not being good enough. Denial of the self. Sexual guilt" (xi). The remedy? To program into one-self these "new thought patterns": "I am part of the Universal design. I am important and I am loved by Life itself. I am powerful and capable. I love and appreciate all of myself" (147).

Because Peter has trouble completely keeping his cool and cannot hide his demagoguery, he draws attention away from another character, Claire (Kate McGregor-Stewart), Wrenwood's director, who herself first came there suffering from hypersensitivity ("Now I'm just semi-hypersensitive like the rest of the world," she jokes). It is Claire who presides over the evening congregations, reiterating "community wishes" ("restraint in sexual interaction" is the main one: "Instead we ask that you try to focus these feelings inward toward your personal growth and self-realization—end of speech!"), welcoming newcomers, and setting the stage for Peter. Seeming a little dazed after her welcome session, Carol wanders back in the dark to her cabin and once inside starts to weep. After a few moments, Claire appears at the door and cautiously enters. In the low, persuasive voice of Iago, she congratulates and comforts Carol with an anecdote: "You know, when I first came here I couldn't even walk. I'd been living six miles from this chemical factory—this was in Michigan—that was leaking like fifteen gallons of chemical by-products every day. When I got here, all I could do was sit in my safe room, and every day, every hour of every day, I would look at myself in the mirror, and I would say to myself: 'Claire, I love you, I really love you.' At the end of the month I could leave my room, and shortly thereafter I was walking. For me this was a gift, this whole thing was a gift, because everything got taken from me—everything in the material world—and what was left was me." So it is Claire who first expresses the self-affirmation that will control Carol at the end of *Safe*. By means of matronly homilies, a pernicious therapeutic doctrine of selfhood extends itself—or inserts itself, finding a way into Carol for the content that the psychiatrist demanded. Big-hearted Claire is a very good transmitter. Her character raises the problem of insidious coercion—power exercised through a hug and coaxing affection—that is also at issue in *Dottie Gets Spanked.*

Carol is lost to Greg and Rory at Wrenwood. She calls and then writes home positively about her gradual progress, but when they come to visit her she is mainly preoccupied with the newly cherished idea of self-motivated slow recovery. Carol asks Claire about the supersafe, igloo-like, porcelain-lined room left vacant by the old man's death, and when, oxygen bottle in hand, she stares expectantly at it, a lesion on her forehead like a circular mark from a branding iron is visible. Greg and an irritable Rory help her move in before they say goodbye. The image of the three of them together is a variation on the out-of-line family. Rory is in the foreground, slightly out of focus, looking at his parents, who face him in the middle ground. This family, unlike Stevie's, is about to break apart irreparably, three splitting up. Whatever resemblances there might have been before, Carol's detachment from her family now could not be more different from Richie's in *Poison*.

Carol and her cooking partner Chris (James LeGros, who will later play Wally in *Mildred Pierce*) make a lasagne dinner. Sitting next to Claire, Peter majestically recounts a dream: "Suddenly all I see, all over my hands and my legs, are . . . black horrible sores all over me, oozing, and at first I'm horrified and I'm, I'm full of self-pity and anger,

I'm enraged—until I realize, suddenly I look down again and I realize that they aren't sores at all, but these . . . black pansies, these sort of wilted black pansies that I used to pick when I was a child. So in my dream I remember that, and, and as I pick up each wilted flower, they would just instantly bloom into beautiful bouquets, every single one!" It is a dream of healing. Rage subsides to self-help serenity; cankers become garlands. Claire immediately approves the way Peter moves from distress to its surmounting, endorsing the therapeutic trajectory: "Ending in rejoice!"

Carol's forehead lesion, her own darkening sore, only develops after she arrives at Wrenwood. What she loses at the same time is her remove and unreadability—her ability to seem to move like a ghost, to fade out of the picture, or to annul an encounter such as the one with the psychiatrist. According to Bersani's reading of *Safe*, Carol demonstrates a "radical aloneness" that is related to her previously awkward, inadequate speech—think of her inability to respond to the lewd joke made by Greg's colleague—"as if the language that makes her a social being were a violation of an intrinsic being-apart and silence" ("Illegitimacy"). When she sits in the upscale shrink's room, she fails to talk as expected—language cannot regulate the occasion.

There is dancing while "Whenever I Call You Friend" by Kenny Loggins (featuring Stevie Nicks) plays. A surprise birthday cake is brought

Self-educated (*Safe*).

out for Carol. She is relaxed and even convivial, and she falteringly starts to speak. Terrible parasitic flower words sprout from the ruins of the self-lessening that might have freed her: "I don't know what I'm saying, it's just that I really hated myself before I came here and, um, so I'm trying to see myself hopefully, um, more as I am, more, um, more positive, like seeing the pluses, like I think it's slowly opening up now, people's minds, like, um, educating and AIDS, um, and other types of diseases. . . ." (She cannot finish, but Peter is there to round things off.)

On what must be her first night in the igloo, whose interior is like an air-raid shelter, she stares into a little mirror on the wall. Finally in closeup, her sickly face mottled and disfigured, Carol again speaks Wrenwood words, this time more confidently, the words Claire transmitted that time in the cabin: "I really love you. I love you."

I'm Now There

In Fassbinder's TV film *Fear of Fear* (1975), Margot (Margit Carstensen) starts to suffer from stifling dread. She stands in front of the bathroom mirror and asks: "What is that, me?" Her husband Kurt (Ulrich Faulhaber), focused on his extramural math study, is dismissive of her complaints of angst: "We'll have lots of time to be happy after my exam," he mutters. She gets Valium from the nearby doctor (Adrian Hoven), who seduces her. Then she takes to drink, which outrages her sister-in-law Lore (Irm Hermann), who screams: "We're the normal ones! And one day, she'll burn the place down, believe me!" Finally Margot is consigned to a clinic, out of which she emerges with a reinforced, compliant sense of identity, of "I": "I have a deep depression, and I need my pills to pull out of it." She shares this reinforced, armored "I" with Effi in *Fontane Effi Briest,* who returns home to die. Effi, who not long before, in her darkest hour, found fine, brave words of rage at her husband and daughter's hypocrisy ("What I did disgusts me, but your virtuousness disgusts me even more"), goes to her death penitent. Maternal solicitude seems to have something like the effect on Effi as pills and therapy do on Margot. "In a way—forgive my saying this now—you really brought your sorrows on yourself," says the mother. Effi consents to the proposition, and more: "During the days I've been ill, which have been almost the loveliest days of my life, I've come to see that [my husband] was right in everything." Haynes's striking development of the theme of female psychic crisis is to subtract desire from it, but the "I" in which Carol speaks at the end of *Safe*—this "I" that is now firmly "in" her—is the same as Margot's and Effi's, obedient and defeated, and it may make a viewer hope in vain for a scene of retaliatory violence like the one in *Jeanne Dielman*, or at least some revived expression of disgust at virtuousness. But no: *Safe* is a tragedy.

In *Fear of Fear*, the possibility of an alternative outcome to Margot's crisis is figured in two ways. There is, first, the character of Herr Bauer (Kurt Raab), called a schizophrenic, who takes a curious, protective interest in Margot before eventually killing himself. He suddenly asks her in the street one time: "Is there someone else you can discuss it with?" Perhaps, together, if they had conferred, she could have avoided the Valium-is-health outcome. The second possibility is figured in a heat-haze editing effect that occasionally makes the surface of the image seem to wobble, as though some transparent wall around Margot were being disturbed, becoming unstable—as though she lived in an observation tank that, if only she knew it, she could break out of. Carol, like Margot, has chances. But she is defeated through language, through learning a new way of talking, and nothing is ever going to breach the walls of her fortified safe room, the materialization of the "in" that the analyst insisted upon. Carol's chances were strange and brief: she seemed capable of what Bersani called "psychic absence" and "refusal to belong," to "shed" identity, not replenish desire and rediscover a confidently health-conscious "I." Walking in the garden at night, she nearly escaped. She nearly disappeared.

In the conclusion to *Red Desert*, Giuliana is strolling with her young son near a factory whose chimneys billow acrid fumes. The boy asks: "Why is the smoke yellow?" She responds: "Because it's poisonous." He continues: "Then if a little bird flies through it, it will die?" She answers: "The birds have learnt that, and they don't fly through it." Then Giuliana leads him by the hand away from the industrial smoke that streams out in the distance behind them. They take the way of safety. Carol does too, having herself contended with toxic fumes that sent her into a panic. It is hard to conceive of her coughing fit in the car as something liberating, yet it costs Carol so much when she stops breaking down.

Velvet Goldmine

Hobgoblins

After glowing love hearts appear in the eyes of Brian Slade (Jonathan Rhys Meyers), which contrast with the methadone-clouded mien of his fellow rock star Curt Wild (Ewan McGregor) sitting across the table, Lou Reed's David Bowie–produced "Satellite of Love" starts to play on the sound track of *Velvet Goldmine* (1998), and the two glam singers are then floating euphorically through the air in what the script calls "neighboring rockets on the Space Spinner ride, reeling over the candy-colored lights of a traveling carnival." It is tempting to enjoy the wonderland realm of Todd Haynes's tribute to glam rock in a similar fashion—to glide between its various comfort zones (country mansion, dollhouse, big top, boudoir) as if this movie were a permissive theme park that combined rollercoaster rides, high-wire acts, and opulently upholstered chambers for voyeurism. *Velvet Goldmine* can seem a pleasure palace, offering viewers the chance to drift in bliss like the onscreen airborne celebrities.

Varda the Message—a vast, votive blog that takes its name from a scrap of polari, the antiquated English gay slang, used in the dialogue—treats *Velvet Goldmine* as if with valentine hearts in its field of vision too. The site free-associatively assembles photos that either count as historical background (publicity shots of Marc Bolan, Alice Cooper, David Bowie, Elvis Presley, Mick Jagger, Lou Reed, Iggy Pop, Roxy Music) or just have some superficial affinity with the *Velvet Goldmine* jamboree. An image only need be theatrical, debonair, haughty, or luxurious to be recruited. Stills from Luchino Visconti's glam-era *Ludwig* (1972) joined the retinue on March 12, 2012, side by side with frame-grabs from Haynes's film. Next to Brian wearing a glittering top hat is an image of Romy Schneider in the role of an empress, wearing grand equestrian headgear in Visconti's account of Bavaria's mad King Ludwig II. These two closeups share an ambience of low-lit aristocratic decadence but little else. Above the stills are two showcards for *Ludwig,* their shared tagline retyped, with a minor alteration, by the blogger: "~~Ludwig~~ Brian Slade. He loved women. He loved men. He lived as controversially as he ruled. But he did not care what the world thought. He was the world." The rule of passing resemblance prevails, one louche aesthete substituting for another with as little effort as it takes to strike through the regal name. The titillating marketing hype is endorsed: narcissistic immersion, bisexuality, thrilling scandal!

It is a wishful-watching version of *Velvet Goldmine*. Haynes's film is a downhearted fantasia in fits and spasms, edited to an unrelenting rhythm that—like the breakdown sequence in *Superstar* and the dreams in *Dottie Gets Spanked*—lacks tranquility, even though some of the film's myriad fragments do depict success and at least a semblance of happiness. If *Velvet Goldmine* is formally hedonistic, it is a hedonism of delirium, adrenaline, and drugs—never more so than in a sequence that cuts between the Mancunian Arthur Stuart (Christian Bale) masturbating feverishly in his bedroom and a rock-star orgy. Varda the Message disavows this montage speed as well. The January 25, 2012, entry compiles three overlapping, cropped, significantly brightened and touched-up mini-clips of Arthur from this scene—just a few frames each, playing back on a loop—and the effect is anesthetic. The sequence's interlaced cruelties are blotted out, and a scene of abjection becomes a blandly erotic triptych. "Varda" means look, but some things are upsetting to observe, and so it is no wonder that one response to *Velvet Goldmine*—at its own often flamboyant invitation—is to enter a daydream mode, enchanted by resemblances and recurrences and star-spangled auditoria, and easily distracted from any anguish leaking through.

Velvet Goldmine is difficult and unyielding whenever the enchantment wears off. Timeframes, storylines, and characters are entwined in a tight braid. The film could be called a hall of mirrors, but it is better described as a labyrinth, arranged on more than one level and full of traps, a condemned edifice in which it is easy to trip or even to fall through the floor. In a rueful sequence, Brian's sacked first manager Cecil (Michael Feast), who is being interviewed by Arthur in a spartan hospital ward, recalls in voiceover the festival at which Brian was first mesmerized by the raucous Curt. There is a flashback-within-a-flashback to an incident in the Michigan-born singer's adolescence. Thirteen-year-old Curt is given electroshock treatment to "fry the fairy clean out of him." It is true that young Curt's brother winks at him as he lies strapped tight to a gurney, but such insouciant gestures in *Velvet Goldmine* struggle to hold their own against counterparts like the hospital image that ends the scene in which Cecil is introduced: an unfurnished, unlit institutional room in which a bereft man in a wheelchair looks out of a window while, behind him, another man sits silently, no trace of glam anywhere. Or the shots of Arthur looking inconsolable—as his fellow passengers do, too—in a dirty subway car in 1984 New York that would not be out of place in Adrian Lyne's psycho-horror film *Jacob's Ladder* (1990).

This condition of loneliness and tribulation is, contrary to Varda the Message, what *Velvet Goldmine* shares with *Ludwig*. Like Visconti's *Death in Venice* (1971), which Haynes's film gestures toward when it uses a snippet of Mahler's Sixth Symphony to accompany a night-club scene, *Ludwig* is a study of psychic meltdown. The king (Helmut Berger) says: "The world around us is unbearable and miserable. Men are only after material security, nothing else. They are ready to lose their lives in order to achieve that. I want to be free! Free to look for unhappiness in the unreachable." He receives a cold reply from Dürckheim (Helmut Griem): "We live in a world where there are no innocents, but he is mistaken if he thinks he can find happiness outside the rules and duties of men. Those who love life cannot afford to search for the unreachable but have to be extremely careful. This is true even for a monarch . . . because the great power that a monarch has is limited by the boundaries of the society of which he is part." Both Ludwig and *Death in Venice*'s Gustav (Dirk Bogarde) seek sanctuary regardless, but to no avail. Black rot creeps into them both. The sovereign's teeth

Subway of sorrow (*Velvet Goldmine*).

decay disgustingly; hair dye trickles down Gustav's face like inky blood. Beneath his opulent palace, the monarch builds a grotto around an underground lake with captive swans; the composer retreats to Venice, where a plague follows him. *Velvet Goldmine* builds grottos too, and they are no more effectual as havens.

This pessimism that infuses Haynes's film is true to the dark side of glam rock. For example, as Ian Penman pointed out in "The Shattered Glass," the initial words of the opening track of the eponymous first Roxy Music album, "Re-Make/Re-Model," undermine the transformer logic of the song title with frustration and obstinacy: "I tried but I could not find a way! / Looking back all I did was look away." Futuristic, flamboyantly mercurial, sybaritic: such characterizations are only part of the story. When Bowie—who refused permission for his music to be used in the film, though the sound track does include his composition for Steve Harley and Cockney Rebel, "Make Me Smile (Come Up and See Me)"—recorded sci-fi concept albums in the mid-1970s, there was an edge of either apocalypticism (*The Rise and Fall of Ziggy Stardust and the Spiders from Mars,* which lachrymosely imagines the world ending in "Five Years") or dystopia (the *1984*-inspired *Diamond Dogs,* whose gatefold artwork is alluded to on the sleeve of *Velvet Goldmine*'s substitute, *The Ballad of Maxwell Demon*). And in the anthemic "Life on Mars?" the notion of interplanetary wonder is framed by the disillusion of a teenager who, as Peter Doggett put it in *The Man Who Sold the World,* "can no longer believe in the fantasies she is being fed" (132). The song may build to the crescendo of its question about extraterrestrial beings, but its "clash of cynical despair and compassionate commitment was almost shocking." In other songs also on the 1971 *Hunky Dory,* anguish predominates—the slow, esoteric, damned "Quicksand," with its cracked delivery of the repeated line "I ain't got the power anymore," and above all "The Bewlay Brothers," a portrait of Bowie's tormented half-brother that culminates in horrible echoey cackles, what Doggett aptly called "a congress of hobgoblins . . . the stuff of nightmares" (130–31). *Hunky Dory* also includes "Changes" on the upbeat, chameleon front, but the album is so weighed down by a consciousness of shifts that cannot be made or the ones that spin off into insanity that nothing escapes the quicksand.

With Roxy Music, *Velvet Goldmine*'s other main English point of reference, there is a different downside. Lead singer Bryan Ferry spins a fantasy of a past libertinism in the kind of cabaret milieu that Roxy Music's songs suggest could exist last night or else a hundred years ago, in which the dissolute, world-weary singer expertly makes his conquests night after night. This is not really the glamour of youth, and the Roxy Music song that is most prominent in *Velvet Goldmine* is "2HB," a languorous tribute to Humphrey Bogart, the quintessential star from the time before teen culture, a specially recorded cover version of which plays powerfully over the film's closing montage. "Long time since we're together," goes this mournful track. "I also took a closer look at Roxy Music," Haynes told Moverman in the "Superstardust" interview published with the *Velvet Goldmine* screenplay, "and found a tremendous sense of mourning, longing, and a general retrospective point of view in all their music. It gives it an implicit melodrama where the emotionality is not lost, despite the excessive statement or gesture. I knew I wanted something like that in the structure of the film, so the narrative could become all about the past and its lost moments" (xiv). The loss is easy to find in such recordings as "Song for Europe"—which laments the passing of "those moments . . . we'll never find again," the world now just "a shell full of memories"—or "Mother of Pearl": "If you're looking for love / in a looking-glass world / it's pretty hard to find." (Both songs appear on *Stranded* from 1973—the first Roxy Music album not to feature Brian Eno.)

It is tainted pain, devious suffering. "This lounge lizard cries crocodile tears on your shoulder," according to Penman: "To begin this seduction, his Roxy is done up to the nines, is shining, obtuse, frantic, resplendent, dramatic, confused, all over the place. But it is most of all *corrupt*: nostalgic, practised, and corrupt" (106). There is hurt and more than a hint of depravity—glam's sideshow of glumness, gloom, and predation.

Perfect and Poisonous

The mischievous prologue to *Velvet Goldmine* combines gay history and space-age fantasy: Oscar Wilde and a UFO. The viewpoint floats down from the wheeling spaceship to discover the future literary star as a wrapped-up foundling on a Dublin doorstep in 1854, a green brooch affixed to his swaddling. At school, Oscar stands up, the brooch now pinning a green silk cravat to his starched collar, and says anachronistically to his class: "I want to be a pop idol" (the bewhiskered schoolmaster seems rather intrigued by the admission). A century later, gray-uniformed schoolboys about the age of *Dottie Gets Spanked*'s Stevie are seen in a crane shot that is as graceful as the bullies in the playground are remorseless. Face down in the dirt, the battered youngster finds Oscar's jewel, and as he first wanders in a studio wood toward a bright sun and then appears in profile painting his lips under a faint blue light, a smooth female voiceover is heard: "Childhood, adults always say, is the happiest time in life, but as long as he could remember Jack Fairy knew better. Until one mysterious day when Jack would discover that somewhere there were others quite like him, singled out for a great gift. And one day the whole stinking world would be theirs." Then Eno's joyous "Needle in the Camel's Eye" from 1973 jolts the sound track into life to accompany the film's Day-Glo title sequence, in which a grownup and made-up Jack (Wicko Westmoreland), wearing a black felt hat and tight-fitting PVC mac with biker detailing, strolls the London streets that throng with exuberant, platform-heeled teenage fans of Brian—one of whom, in a green velvet frock coat, is Arthur.

The sassy opening minutes of *Velvet Goldmine* immediately complicate their own celebration of the spangled pop world by showing Jack on his own. (The character was inspired by the filmmaker Jack Smith.) He cuts an enigmatic, solitary figure throughout the film. It seems that he has not found "others quite like him," and indeed the boys who beat him up at school could easily be among the zestful running teenagers. Mock-documentary clips raise the issue directly. "At the moment, having a gay image is the in thing," says one gruff musician, but then Curt utters cautionary words: "But you just can't fake being gay, you know. If you're gonna claim that you're gay, you're gonna have to make love in gay style, and most of these kids just aren't gonna make it. That line—'everyone's bisexual'—is a very popular thing to say right now, but personally I think it's meaningless." Another complicating element of *Velvet Goldmine* is a whole litany of slurs tainting the ebullient sex-and-gender experimentation elsewhere: *woofter, shirt-lifter, maricon, épicène,* and so on.

At the concert Arthur and the others are rushing to, the fans witness the hoax assassination of Slade's blue-haired Maxwell Demon persona (modeled on Ziggy Stardust) as he stands gleamingly onstage in his silver bodysuit accessorized with a diamond choker and feathered headdress.

The March 17, 1974, Sunday *Observer* Arthur studies alone in a row-house doorway leads with the Slade-slaying story, and then another rising crane shot completes the sequence's move from convivial fans adoring a star in all his pomp to a morning-after solitary experience of loss.

If this Chinese box of a film's outermost frame is the brooch-and-spaceship fairy tale—the narrator resumes after the stage death, speaking of an "unknown land" of possibility and artifice, "full of strange flowers and subtle perfumes, a land of which it is joy of all joys to dream, a land where all things are perfect and poisonous"—the frame-within-the-frame is Arthur's quest on the anniversary of the hoax, in 1984, to unravel the enduring enigma of Brian. By this time, short-haired Arthur is a journalist for the *New York Herald*; he has retained his northern accent but now wears a shapeless dark polo shirt. When his editor makes the assignment, Arthur is unenthusiastic. "I want you because you remember," says the boss, but the drab, pensive reporter gives no hint of how much. The city is also colorless and dreary, a dystopian metropolis that contrasts with the earlier vision of bright, bustling London. Loudspeakers urge pedestrians to join civic groups. Armed men in black uniforms stand on the street. There are what look like bread lines. A giant outdoor screen beams out a concert by Tommy Stone (Alastair Cumming), a stadium-rock god who thanks sponsors and a presidential committee for enabling the satellite broadcast. Arthur's voiceover is despondent: "Suddenly I was being paid to remember all the things that money, the future, and the serious life made so certain that I'd forget." From whatever further temporal distance Arthur remembers the assignment, he adds: "Clearly there was something, something from the past spooking me back. I didn't realize at the time that it was you." On the way into the subway he thinks he sees Curt going the other way.

Arthur interviews both Cecil, whose story ends with being unceremoniously dumped when the singer gets a better offer from Jerry Devine (Eddie Izzard), and Brian's ex-wife Mandy (Toni Collette), who has been reduced to performing in dives as the Divine Miss Mandy Slade. Her testimony is bitter, too: "Right after everything crashed we split, and Brian—he just became someone else. But then again he always was." She recalls the Sombrero Club in West London on New Year's Eve 1969, where she first met Brian, still learning the clubland ropes, with "the feeling in the air that anything was possible."

A whirlwind romance begins, though not an exclusive one: Brian is seen hungrily kissing Jack too. Mandy delights in Brian's provocative confession of bisexuality at a scandalous 1972 press conference for *The Ballad of Maxwell Demon,* which takes the singer further on his way to becoming what Jerry calls a "space-age fucking superstar."

It is the collaboration with Curt that launches Brian into the stratosphere. The two men kiss for press cameras, and publication of the scandalous image is the apogee of the hype. But in a montage accompanied by a cover version of another Eno track, "Baby's on Fire," whose instrumentation includes a kind of speeded-up warning siren, the cost of the spectacle is made visible. At an orgiastic party where everyone is wasted, Brian and Curt go off together, watched resentfully by Brian's wardrobe assistant Shannon (Emily Woof) and Mandy. "It's funny how beautiful people look when they're walking out the door," Mandy tells Arthur. It is the beginning of the end not only for the Slades' showbiz marriage but also for the collaboration between the English and American stars, as a result of Curt's increasingly erratic and aggressive behavior (he smashes up a studio in a rage). "It all came crashing down," Mandy recalls. Curt heads for Berlin, but after-the-party angst is most keenly evident when Brian and Mandy discuss their impending divorce while he snorts coke off another woman in a hotel bedroom. Distraught, she starts shouting at the addled singer—"Your problem is you get what you want and do what you will!"—which has the effect of summoning the odiously officious Shannon. She shows the starmaker the door while Brian sputters with drug-hyped glee.

Brian's final interview before his editor nixes the story is less productive. He calls Curt from a pay phone and is told, "I don't know who the hell gave you this number, but Curt Wild is not available, not interested in granting you or anybody else an interview on this subject. You got it?" It is left to Arthur to join the dots between Brian and Tommy. Toward the end of *Velvet Goldmine,* the New York storyline is given a conspiracy twist. Mysterious dark-suited men appear to discourage Curt from giving Arthur an interview about Brian. Arthur's computer check on possible name-changes by Brian yields nothing: "°°ACCESS DENIED°°" flashes on the screen. Then he sees Tommy on TV and recognizes the ever-ambitious Shannon speaking at the singer's press conference. A database search reveals that Brian was christened Thomas Brian Stoningham Slade—which gets very near to "Tommy Stone" when "Brian Slade" is knocked out. Arthur rushes to the newsroom, only to be told by the *Herald* editor that the story has been dropped. The men in suits have done their work on behalf of this superstar functionary. Arthur hangs at the back of another press conference (at which Tommy praises the president) and shouts a question about Brian. Shannon shuts the whole thing down.

Vignette flashbacks to Arthur's unhappy adolescence punctuate *Velvet Goldmine*. The excitement of buying *The Ballad of Maxwell Demon* is offset by the scorn of his tough-guy brother (Ryan Pope) in the record shop—"Bloody Nora, our kid's one of them pansy rockers" ("He's a fucking poof, that one there," remarks the brother's friend, referring to Brian)—and the seething disapproval of his parents. Mr. Stuart (Jim Whelan) has a history of bad temper, or so it would seem from the fact that Mrs. Stuart (Sylvia Grant) asks with alarm when her husband storms up to Arthur's room because of the loud music, "Jim, what are you gonna do? Jim!" When he discovers his son kneeling over a homoerotic music-magazine image (based on Mick Rock's famous photo of Bowie in blow-job posture before Mick Ronson's electric guitar), he is apoplectic: "You bring shame to your mother and me: it's a shameful, filthy thing you're doing—do you hear me?!" When Mrs. Stuart comes upstairs, they are assembled as an out-of-line family ready to break apart. In the background, Arthur is in front of his mirror, hunching over as he starts to sob. His father commands him to stand up. His mother looms in the foreground, all three of them facing away from camera until Mr. Stuart in between the other two turns to walk out, leaving the teenager in humiliation. There follows an image as painful as any other in Haynes's films: a closeup of Arthur reflected in the mirror, crying, shaking with anguish, with what looks like a faint mist of blood below his left nostril.

Brian's family life ends on the bus he takes to London. In the capital he makes friends with a glam band, the Flaming Creatures, and eventually attends both the fake-assassination gig and the Death of Glitter concert. The surprise sprung at the end of *Velvet Goldmine* is a scene in which, after the latter performance, Arthur is picked up by Curt. Home-movie-style footage shows them shirtless and relaxed in the open air, but when they meet again in 1984, backstage at the Tommy Stone stadium show, it is hard to tell who remembers what about the carefree rooftop lovemaking of the final flashback.

Bedroom Encounters

Glam rock theatrically brought to the mainstream a countercultural disdain for the tawdriness and psychopathologies of everyday life. Pageantry and liberating pretense could rule instead, in keeping with Genet's advice in "Le Funambule": "Love the circus and despise the world." In his preface to Barney Hoskyns's *Glam!* Haynes wrote: "[F]or a brief time pop culture would proclaim that identities and sexualities were not stable things but quivery and costumed, and rock and roll would paint its face and turn the mirror around, inverting in the process everything in sight" (xi).

Glam therefore had an affinity with the endeavor by radical gay writers in the 1970s to reimagine social relations—to turn them around and upside-down—from the perspective of what Guy Hocquenghem in *Homosexual Desire* called "the non-sublimated homosexual," the "social misfit in the heterosexual family society" (109). Something else could replace this society—for example, a "horizontal" arrangement that does not derive from father-to-son generational hierarchy: "[T]he homosexual points the way to another possible form of relationship which we hardly dare call 'society.'" There could be a transformation of desire. John Rechy in *The Sexual Outlaw* celebrated promiscuity, oppositional desire unbound and perpetually replenished: "Promiscuous homosexuals (outlaws with dual identities—tomorrow they will go to offices and construction sites) are the shock troops of the sexual revolution. The streets are the battleground, the revolution is the sexhunt, a radical statement is made each time a man has sex with another on a street" (299). Hocquenghem's program in *The Screwball Asses* was more total: "Desire must be allowed to function on any object. And not only on one body instead of two or more, simultaneously. And not only on the age class of youth or on the esthetic class of beauty, the formal elements of the class struggle. And not only on one of the two phantasmatic modalities of masochism or masochism disguised as sadism. And not only on one of the two sexes. And not only, assuming these differentiations will eventually disappear, on the human species" (61).

Near the start of the New Queer Cinema forerunner Jennie Livingstone's 1990 documentary about drag balls, *Paris Is Burning*, a man explains the experience of entering a New York venue: "It's like crossing into the looking glass in Wonderland. You go in there and you feel—you feel 100 percent right being gay. . . . It's not what it's like in the world, you know. It should be like that in the world." Is a better and queerer looking-glass world—or antiworld—also imagined in *Velvet Goldmine*? Is it a utopian film? Its music-business grottos are not happy places, and certainly not egalitarian ones—Shannon may thrive, staying by Brian's side as he adopts a new and much more lucrative persona, but neither Cecil nor Mandy do, and what happens to Jerry is unclear. If there is a dimension of pop-culture liberation, it must involve not the pop idols themselves but their fans, and on this point *Velvet Goldmine* is no better than equivocal. The scene preceding Mr. Stuart's outburst typifies the ambiguity. Brian gives the brazen press conference at which he impishly concurs with a journalist's description of him as "a blinking fruit." It is all watched on TV by Arthur and his parents. As soon as Brian says to the journalist, "It wouldn't be the wrong impression in the slightest," Arthur leaps from where he has been sitting like Stevie right in front of the set and proclaims, overjoyed, "That is me—that's me, that—that's me!" But then it becomes apparent that in the film's story this never happened. The next shot shows Arthur still sitting quietly, keeping his enthusiasm and recognition private. He does not ebulliently come out—and had he made this impulsive disclosure, what kind of coming out would it have been anyway? Arthur's sexuality is an enigma. However, during his interview with Mandy, something unmistakable flickers between the two dejected interlocutors. "I don't think I have what you're looking for," she says as the questions about Brian continue. "I think you do, actually," he says, starting to smile. Despite herself, Mandy smiles too: "Oh yeah, and what makes you think so?" In the sweetest moment of the whole film—and one that is not utopian at all—Arthur answers, "That smile, for one thing," and they are both free of all their troubles for the second it takes for Mandy to short-circuit the flirtation by saying, "Smiles lie."

Fandom comes self-reflexively to the fore in a scene in which two girls (whose faces are never seen) play with Brian and Curt dolls. "My career was on the skids, mate, and you fished me out of the muck—you got me back on my feet, you did," says the girl holding the Curt doll.

Fan fiction (*Velvet Goldmine*).

"It was nothing, chum," says the other. "I wanted to help you make more of that far-out sound. I love your music, my son, and I love—." The Curt doll's ventriloquist spares blushes: "You don't have to say it, mate," and the girls tip the dolls romantically to the floor. Haynes said to Moverman: "I completely agree with you that the doll scene in *Velvet Goldmine*—which is definitely a homage to myself (somebody's got to do it)—does represent the film as a whole, and maybe in the most complete way. A lot of it has to do with the game of laughing and feeling aware of the construct—in a fun way, not in a Brechtian, didactic way" ("Superstardust" xx). Yet laughter and play are so often submerged or left behind in this film, perhaps only in dollhouse safety—only in a world that shuts out the lonely Sunday-morning street, the miserable subway car, and other unhappy fictional locales—can the laughter and role-play of this gay puppetry predominate. Though Haynes refers jokingly to his own homage to *Superstar*, what is so evidently missing from this mini-*Superstar* (but not from other parts of *Velvet Goldmine*) is that earlier film's preoccupation with trauma and isolation. Ensconced in their safe house, the rock-star dolls have nothing to do but canoodle, whereas Karen is menaced beyond endurance. This colorful bedroom is a comfort zone that is hard to take seriously if Mr. Stuart's morality lecture is ever allowed back into the picture.

Many others followed the onscreen girls' lead. *Velvet Goldmine* has inspired an archive of fan or "slash" fiction—Web-published homoerotic (even X-rated) stories involving the characters, often written pseudonymously by young women and collected on sites like Satellite of Love (satellite.shriftweb.org) and www.fanfiction.net. The stories, testament to the film's cult following, are categorized—"Hurt/Comfort," "Romance/Angst," "Angst/Romance," "Suspense"—and range in length from a couple of hundred words to several thousands (a few are even novel-length). One of their generic characteristics is a scenario of immersion, of cocooning and out-of-time couplings. "I kissed you back, not even caring that people were staring at us. There *was* no one else there. There was only *us*" (Silk, "Subtle Innuendo," Satellite of Love); "One evening swaddled in something larger than you or anyone or anything else, one evening where all worries and cares are erased completely. One evening spent erasing everything past, good and bad, for a sleepy foetal feeling nothing else can begin to compare to" (Yesido, "Walk Away," www.fanfiction.net); "The room was suddenly blissfully silent as they kissed, everything and everyone else unimportant" (Lily Stargazer, "Hotels and Limousines," Satellite of Love).

These playing-it-gay escapist fictions of innocent seclusion are in the tradition of fan-penned romances between *Star Trek*'s Captain Kirk and Mr. Spock studied by Constance Penley in *NASA/TREK,* which also sentimentalized homosexuality: "There is a perfectly understandable idealization of the gay male couple in this fan writing, because such a couple, after all, is one in which love and work can be shared by two equals (a state of affairs the fans feel to be almost unattainable for a heterosexual couple). But there is also a comprehension of the fact that *all* men (and women) must be able to recognize their own homosexual tendencies if they are to have any hope of fundamentally changing oppressive sexual roles" (130–31). A link can be made between what Penley saw as the utopianism at work in these romantic fictions and the earlier instances of queer futurology—especially in the idea of a homosexuality shared by everyone that could be the basis of new social relations—as well as glam, but the utopianism has shrunk to fit a therapeutic fan playroom. The diminishment in ambition is in itself very sad, and it resonates with Haynes's account of glam's fate in the Hoskyns preface: "It couldn't last.

The 1980s were on their way—and with them, an overall retreat from the kinds of socio-political inversions that made glam rock possible in the first place. With few exceptions, glam would ultimately fall through the cracks of pop-cultural memory, dispersed and absorbed by gay disco and straight heavy metal, and punctuated by Bowie and Lou Reed's apparent disavowal of their homosexual pasts. Glam rock would become inconsequential to a world of restored binaries and boundaries, a world of men and women, straights and gays, and nothing of interest in between" (xi).

Yet a further problem is that it is debatable, given scenes like the one with Mr. Stuart, or Brian's farewell to Mandy, whether *Velvet Goldmine* ever shows the world turned upside-down and binary-free. For, not only is the film not utopian in the sense of contemplating a through-the-looking-glass future of liberation, but its visions of the past are like quicksand.

Curtains

There are hollowed-out, trinketized references to two Ophuls films in *Velvet Goldmine. Lola Montès* (1955) is recalled when Brian appears dressed as a circus ringmaster and chandeliers are winched up in the "Tumbling Down" sequence. But both times the singer is imperiously striking a pose: he is star and ringmaster, so Ophuls's concern with a performer's exploitation and collusion disappears. The emerald brooch that passes from character to character (ending up in Arthur's pint glass) alludes to the jewelry in *The Earrings of Madame de . . .* (1953). Again, much gets lost in the translation. In Ophuls's tragic love story, the earrings become symbols of the intense love that Louise (Danielle Darrieux) feels for a diplomat, Fabrizio (Vittorio De Sica). By way of punishment for taking permissible flirtation into the realm of unyielding devotion, her husband André (Charles Boyer) humiliates her by forcing her to give away the earrings. When it is clear that she still resists his authority, André is rattled: "I'm sorry for you. You are ill. You are confused. You are trying to transform your regrets into memories." He almost pleads with her: "There is still time. Don't escape this way into sickness and silence." *Velvet Goldmine* has no obvious equivalent of this sangfroid and none of the emotional grandeur of Louise's subsequent martyrdom—certainly not in these scenes that allude in this rather bogus fashion to *Lola Montès* and *The Earrings of Madame de. . . .* When Brian humiliates Mandy with his coked-up laughter, his nasty, erratic narcissism is a world away from André's ice-cold cruel decorum. Yet, in other scenes, Haynes's film depicts an amorous pain just as severe and depressing in its own way—and as bitterly futile—as Louise's obstinate passion for the ultimately unattainable Fabrizio. *Velvet Goldmine* does what Louise is warned against and turns regrets into memories.

The film moves through various scenarios of betrayal and failure, but it heads for a scene of apparent consolation. Arthur strikes gold. In the "Behind the Glam and Glitter" documentary on the Film 4 DVD of *Velvet Goldmine,* Haynes said: "I wanted to bury the past in the film, and so there would be this nostalgia and the sense of something dangerous and exciting that was closed up, that Arthur . . . has to dig out." Glam may have failed to change the world, as 1984 New York proves, but at least there is the reward offered by Arthur's rooftop tryst with Curt. Haynes told Moverman: "[H]e got to sleep with Curt Wild—something most of us don't get to do." But is it certain that this did happen, especially given the problem of unreliable evidence raised in the scene in which the Stuarts watch Brian's press conference?

In anticipation of the longer clip of them in the closing "2HB" sequence, grainy film shows Curt fooling around with Arthur on an old mattress placed on a rooftop. It belongs to a series of gay encounters that *Velvet Goldmine* presents as home movies. The first shot is the introduction to Cecil. Just before he appears in the hospital, there is a brief, grainy Super 8 flashback clip of him and Brian in bed together: accentuating a sense of found-footage authenticity, the camera wildly zooms in and then out, Cecil putting up his hand in the gesture used to ward off a paparazzo. The series resumes just before the doll scene with another intrusive-seeming shot, this time of Brian and Curt. The impression of filming without permission is conveyed when Curt turns to the camera, registers its presence, jeers defiantly, and then throws his champagne glass in its direction. Once more, the home-movie look is associated with access to superstar privacy. The third instance occurs after the collaboration between Brian and Curt reaches its angry conclusion. Recalling the bohemian London of *Performance* (dirs. Donald Cammell and Nicolas Roeg, 1970), the Englishman slightly opens the upstairs net curtains of a grand townhouse to watch Curt getting into a white Rolls-Royce before driving away. "Well this is such a sad affair, / I've opened up my heart," sings Radiohead's Thom Yorke on the Venus in Furs' cover version of Roxy Music's "Bitter-Sweet." Then, abruptly, the world outside the slightly windblown curtains changes, and the image beyond them is again Super 8: on what looks like a beach, the two miniaturized, doll-like rock stars embrace. (This shot was not envisaged in the script.) A closer image of this same between-drapes, false-quotes embrace flashes up right before the grainy clip of Arthur and Curt rolling on the mattress.

Roxy Music's "2HB" (represented in the film by another Venus in Furs cover version) begins with the lines, "Oh I was moved by your screen dream / Celluloid pictures of living," and given the image-crash appearance of this sweet idyll between the embedded frame of the net curtains, it is almost impossible to regard these home movies as sneak peeks into celebrity romance. They are screen dreams, rear projections. Instead of representing a bygone moment of unpolluted fondness shared by Brian and Curt, the beach scene is a convenient remedial—or cynical—vision that Brian reflexively dreams up as a fictive instant response to Curt's departure. And if Super 8 is hard to believe on this occasion, then why rely upon it when it includes Cecil or Arthur? Non-stars, they share a 1984 dolefulness that is good enough reason to soften the past not with misty seaside idylls but with star-fucking fictions.

Such an interpretation of *Velvet Goldmine*'s doubtful Super 8 makes a melancholy sense out of the reality games in Haynes's films

Screen dream (*Velvet Goldmine*).

that could otherwise be seen as postmodern—or indeed glam (in its transformative mode)—pastiche. Haynes's multistory fictions tend to blur reality and fantasy. One of the schoolteachers in "Hero" mentions something that might make Richie's climactic flight just a figment of Felicia's imagination: "It's very odd, but Mrs. Beacon's account of Richie's disappearance—you know, him killing his father and flying away—came directly from one of his stories." And, during the *Dottie Gets Spanked* commentary, Haynes quotes from his original pitch to the producers: "The film should absolutely resist emphasizing the notion of real life versus the imaginary realm: each world should haunt the other, for there are powerful fictions being created on both sides." The *Velvet Goldmine* Blu-ray commentary reiterates: "The idea . . . was to create a world in which reality, fantasy, and memory each have equal weight." But what a horribly sad affair it is, as the song has it, for fantasy and memory to take each other's place.

The past is restaged as a sentimental masque—or even as an outdated vaudeville routine. In an early scene, recalled again by Cecil, seven-year-old Brian (Callum Hamilton) goes to a London music hall to visit his disreputable uncle. Velvet drapes hang on either side of the stage, but there is something else behind them, marked "SAFETY CURTAIN," that protects against fire. The Super 8 trysts in *Velvet Goldmine* are not remembered events that bring consolation in lonely lives: they are safety-curtain fictions of long-ago, oh-so-far-away phantom homosexuality—imaginary films concocted from regret, memorials to what never happened, not to what did. They screen off a dead emptiness.

The intense distress and loss implicit in these unreliable home movies, rather than the teenage fans' doll dramaturgy, associate *Velvet Goldmine* most strongly with *Superstar*. The screen dreams of Cecil and Arthur are fan fictions too, but ones with no trace of utopianism. The Super 8 shots always have the context of loss without a compensating nostalgic overvaluation of past happiness—because that bygone contentment is a counterfeit, and not one that is truly believed to be anything else by its forgers, judging by the somber faces of the characters in 1984. The home-movie shots therefore recall the gulf between the song "Groupie" and its reworking by the Carpenters as "Superstar." The original is a song of woeful reminiscence, while the Carpenters' reworking, divested of the one-night stand that makes narrative sense of it but infused in the vocal performance with an unprecedented far-gone despair, is something much more desolate: a song that mourns nonexperience—missed opportunities transformed into ghost memory, hallucination. The difference between wistful remembrance of things past and regrets turned into sham memories is profound and agonizing . . . at least until some future glam revolution finally cancels out the loneliness and grief that haunt the outskirts of the *Velvet Goldmine* fairground—or until real and virtual become undistinguishable in a new, cybernetic Varda the Message world.

Is there anything at all that ameliorates Haynes's film? There is this: after his father rages at Arthur, the teenager leaves home. The family line disintegrates. Arthur gets on a bus to London. Just in time, before the vehicle leaves, Mrs. Stuart, who said nothing while her husband shamed Arthur, runs around the corner to see him one more—one last—time and wave an ungainly goodbye. She ends up in the middle of the frame as the shaky camera departs with the bus, the unsteady framing suddenly recalling the leave-taking in "Hero."

At the start of *Velvet Goldmine,* words appear on a black screen: "Although what you are about to see is a work of fiction, it should nevertheless be played at maximum volume"—but, in contrast to all the noise of the glam carnival, Arthur's flight from home is peaceful and full of possibility because it occurs in total silence. The journey that he begins on the getaway bus will take him as far as New York, which means that it leads also to the subway of sorrow, but it is further than anyone ever went riding a Space Spinner.

Far from Heaven

The Bird Cage

All of Haynes's films, apart from *Dottie Gets Spanked,* deal with marriage breakdowns. Karen and Tom in *Superstar* barely get started before it is over. Felicia's affair with José in "Hero"—a gardener like *Far from Heaven*'s Raymond Deagan (Dennis Haysbert)—is the last straw for Fred. Carol and Greg in *Safe* drift far apart. Brian and Mandy's *Velvet Goldmine* wedlock ends with the rock star's addled, contemptuous heckling. Robbie and Claire divorce in *I'm Not There* (2007).

Mildred Pierce begins with the separation of Mildred and Bert (Brían F. O'Byrne). Such crises and splits are less common in the Hollywood melodramas that Haynes remodels in *Far from Heaven*. It is true that the wife played by Barbara Stanwyck in Sirk's *All I Desire* (1953) runs away from her duties for a whole decade, but she returns contrite, and the family is restored. Duty is triumphant, and stoical acceptance with a touch of masochism is the usual attitude in these films. Resignation takes on tragic proportions in Ophuls's *The Reckless Moment* (1949), in which Lucia (Joan Bennett), whose husband is away for work, falls for the soft-hearted blackmailer Martin (James Mason). "You don't know how a family can surround you at times," she tells him. Martin replies: "You're quite a prisoner, aren't you?" In the end, he kills a man to protect the institution, and afterward this odd couple stands in agony in her yard, planning how to cover it up, which will finally involve Lucia leaving Martin to die. (The yard scene is echoed near the end of *Far from Heaven*.)

By contrast with frantic family defense, the breakups in Haynes's films might seem to offer extrication from the predicament of domestic melodrama that Haynes described in his director's statement for *Far from Heaven* (included in the *Three Screenplays* volume): "[W]omen"—and not only women—"locked up in houses who emerge, in the end, as lesser human beings for all they surrender to the ways of the world" (xiii). Elmer Bernstein's hopeful tune for the film's finale, which shows Cathy Whitaker (Julianne Moore) apparently resilient after her own marriage dissolution, is called "Beginnings," but has she truly avoided surrender and capture as her forebears in Hollywood melodrama could not? Or are the locks still where they always were?

In *The Time of the Assassins: A Study of Rimbaud*, a book that was a source for Haynes's Brown University graduation film, *Assassins: A Film Concerning Rimbaud* (1985), Henry Miller quoted a letter Vincent Van Gogh wrote his brother Theo in July 1880: "And men are often prevented by circumstances from doing things, a prisoner in I do not know what horrible, horrible, most horrible cage. There is also, I know it, the deliverance, the tardy deliverance. A just or unjustly ruined reputation, poverty, fatal circumstances, adversity, that is what it is that keeps us shut in, confines us, seems to bury us, but, however, one feels certain barriers, certain gates, certain walls" (63). In the original context, the three-times-horrible enclosure was located in a nursery setting. Van Gogh elaborated: "But then the season of the great migration arrives: an attack of melancholy. He has everything he needs, say the children who tend him in his cage—but he looks out, at the heavy thundery sky, and in his heart of hearts he rebels against his fate. I am caged, I am caged and you say I need nothing, you idiots! I have everything I need, indeed! Oh, please give me the freedom to be a bird like other birds" (74). The desire is evoked for a liberation that can only be achieved if access can be gained to a visible though cut-off outside world, but in the context of Haynes's films, such a scenario is not simple. In *Superstar,* there is Karen's exit from a claustrophobic family home to consider, which leads only to a worse sense of acrimonious claustrophobia than before. There are, as well, the masochistic Borstal games in "Homo" that start to give inmates an incentive to acclimatize—even, in the manner of so-called Stockholm Syndrome, to adjust to their situation enthusiastically. And there is the resemblance between Van Gogh's nursery and the playing-with-dolls scene in *Velvet Goldmine.*

In Sirk's *There's Always Tomorrow* (1956), an unhappy husband, Clifford (Fred MacMurray), is a toymaker. He says to his wife Marion (Joan Bennett): "I'm tired of the children taking over. I'm tired of being pushed in the corner, of being taken for granted. . . . I'm becoming like one of my toys: Clifford Groves the Walkie-Talkie Robot. Wind me up in the morning and I walk and talk, I go to work all day. Wind me up again and I come home at night and eat dinner and go to bed. . . . I'm not talking about expenses, I'm talking about life—my life, our life. I'm sick and tired of the sameness day in and day out. Don't you ever want to get out of this house, go some place, move around?" It turns out that Marion does not. She replies lightheartedly: "I'm constantly moving around, that's how I keep my figure, what with running the house and looking after the children." Clifford feels trapped, but the familiar household flow is motion enough for Marion. At the end of the film, Clifford is viewed through a window frame at home as he watches, with an expression of hopelessness, an airplane flying overhead. This bird is staying in his cage. "I'm alright now," he says, when Marion expresses concern at his recent irritability. "You know me better than I know myself," he continues, and she replies warmly, "I should, after a lifetime with you," which is the sort of tomorrowless phrase people use when somebody is either very old or dead.

A Small Town in New England

The camera is high up in the trees. It is fall 1957 in Hartford, Connecticut, and people are walking in the square outside the train station. Bernstein's title theme has layers of suggestion: the oboe introducing the melody is tentative, even reproachful, and there is a hint of menace and suspense in the string section's part. These troubling elements are swept away by the the brass instruments' yearning consolidation of the melody as the title appears onscreen in pale blue cursive lettering (the words were painted and then digitally superimposed). Cathy picks up her daughter Janice (Lindsay Andretta) from dance class, then drives to their spacious whitewashed house. Both Janice's brother David (Ryan Ward) and the housekeeper Sybil (Viola Davis) are waiting. Sybil scoops up grocery bags from the trunk. Cathy's friend Eleanor Fine (Patricia Clarkson) arrives, and indoors the two women look at color samples. They are planning the annual party for their husbands' advertising firm, Magnatech.

Like a DJ remixing a dozen tracks, or perhaps like Victor Frankenstein stitching together a body out of fragmentary parts, Haynes's film is made out of bits. The main sources are *The Reckless Moment, Fear Eats the Soul,* and Sirk's *All That Heaven Allows* (1955), in which a widow, Cary (Jane Wyman), falls in love with a gardener decades younger than her, Ron (Rock Hudson), and incurs the wrath of her nearly grown children and the disapproval of neighbors. Another significant predecessor is the neo-noir remake of *The Reckless Moment* directed by Scott McGehee and David Siegel, *The Deep End* (2001), which adds a gay son to the story.

Haynes's allusions have varying degrees of directness. Sometimes the association is vague, as with the way the Magnatech office is slightly reminiscent of the workplace in *Written on the Wind.* On other occasions, the incorporation is more like direct quotation. When Cathy, wearing a headscarf, stands on the station platform to wave to Raymond, it closely resembles a scene near the end of Sirk's *A Time to Love and a Time to Die* (1958). Or take the Whitaker children. Cathy fusses about David's lack of clothing ("Where's your jacket?"), recalling a running joke in *The Reckless Moment* ("Put on your shirt, David"). In the next scene, Janice tells her mother, "When I grow up . . . I hope I look exactly as pretty as you," repeating the daughter's words in *There's Always Tomorrow*: "I hope I look as pretty as mother when I grow up." Just as often, though, Haynes splices together more than one source. So Raymond combines aspects of Ali in *Fear Eats the Soul*, Ron in *All That Heaven Allows*, and Martin in *The Reckless Moment*; Sybil is named for the housekeeper in *The Reckless Moment* but also resembles Annie (Juanita Moore) in Sirk's *Imitation of Life* (1959); Raymond's daughter is Sarah (Jordan Puryear), invoking the name of Annie's unhappy daughter, Sarah Jane (played by two actresses, Karin Dicker and Susan Kohner).

That evening, a phone call comes from the police department: Cathy's husband Frank (Dennis Quaid) has been arrested for loitering, and she has to collect him. The Whitakers' apparently idyllic, prosperous life is being shaken. The next morning, while she is giving an interview to a writer from the *Hartford Weekly Gazette*, Cathy is surprised to see a tall black man outside. He introduces himself as Raymond, the son of the Whitakers' regular gardener, who has died. (He later explains that he is a widower.)

Hartford has a dingy sexual underworld. After drinks with coworkers, Frank mooches over to Fabian's Ritz cinema, where men cruise each other on the stairs, the mise-en-scène inspired by Edward Hopper's *New York Movie*. Frank's next stop is a gay bar lit the color of slime. Another evening, he calls to say that he is working late—"Father never wants to come home," says Janice—and on impulse Cathy decides to deliver his meal. At the office, she is shocked to find him kissing a man he met at the bar. Frank gruffly discloses at home later that he "once, a long time ago . . . had problems" but "just figured that was it."

The couple go to the town plaza for an appointment with Dr. Bowman (James Rebhorn), but the psychiatrist asks Cathy to wait outside. This levelheaded physician is candid with his patient: "Today the general attitude regarding this sort of behavior is naturally more modern, more scientific than it ever has been before. But for those who do seek treatment, who possess the will and desire to lead a normal life, there still remains only a scant 5 to 30 percent rate of success for complete heterosexual conversion." Frank agrees to attend psychiatric sessions: "I can't let this thing destroy my life, my family's life. I know it's a sickness because it makes me feel despicable. I promise you, Dr. Bowman, I'm going to beat this thing." Outside, Frank is overwhelmed with discomfort, and he turns on his supportive spouse: "I just wanna get the whole fucking thing over with! Can you understand that?!"

There is now a whole new side to the model couple, and someone other than Cathy might not have stayed so cool when Eleanor later mentions a friend's "flowery" art-dealer uncle, who is "light on his feet" and "one of those." She adds, "Call me old-fashioned, I just like all the men I'm around to be all men." Cathy is good at putting on a brave face, and that night, when Frank deflects her questions about his latest visit to Dr. Bowman, she keeps things light and conventional: "Oh Frank, wait till you see the hors d'oeuvres! The caterer's doing just such a marvelous job. I think you're going to be so pleased this year, darling, I really do."

Cathy makes small talk with Eleanor, Mona Lauder (Celia Weston), and her flouncing uncle, Maurice Farnsworth (J. B. Adams), at the opening of the postimpressionist art exhibit at the Hartford Cultural Center—but it is Raymond, attending with Sarah, who shows the keenest and best-informed appreciation of the work, discussing Joan Miró's *The Nightingale's Song at Midnight and the Morning Rain* enthusiastically with Cathy. Sarah goes to play outside with three boys who treat her meanly. The ill treatment is less blatant inside, but the spiteful looks Mona and Maurice give Cathy and Raymond are unambiguously disapproving. "You certainly seem on familiar terms with him," says Eleanor.

Art lovers (*Far from Heaven*).

At the Magnatech party, Frank gets drunk. After the guests have left, he makes a move on Cathy in the blue-lit front room and then recoils. "Frank, Frank, you're all man to me, you're all man," she says, and his rage boils over: he strikes her. The next day she starts to weep in the garden, initially not noticing Raymond, who invites her on a trip to collect shrubs on the outskirts of town. They walk and talk, and then go for a drink at a bar frequented by blacks, where they dance (as Emmi and Ali do in *Fear Eats the Soul*). Mona happens to observe them going in, and soon gossip spreads. Eleanor warns Cathy about it (Mona "has been on some kind of rampage"), and Frank makes the most of the role-reversal by haranguing his wife pompously.

After Christmas, the spouses try to start fresh by going on holiday. They seem relaxed at New Year's Eve dinner in Miami, though Frank's gaze is caught for a moment by a fair-haired young man (Nicholas Joy), who smiles at him. The two spot each other again across the pool, and the youngster follows Frank back to his room. A little while after their return to Hartford, he tells Cathy what has happened: "I've fallen in love with someone who wants to be with me. Oh Cathy. I, I just, I, I never knew what it felt like, but, I know that sounds so cruel, but. Oh God, Cathy, I tried, I tried so hard to make it go away. I thought that I could do it for you and for the kids. But I can't, I just, I can't!" Cathy confides in Eleanor, mentioning that she had been able to talk about her unhappiness to Raymond—"We would just talk, and somehow it made me feel, I don't know, alive somewhere," which begs the question of how she usually feels—and all of a sudden the previously sympathetic Eleanor is as cold as ice.

Weeks after it happened, Cathy finds out from Sybil that while she and Frank were in Florida, Sarah was assaulted (another repercussion of Mona's gossip). Cathy goes right away to see the Deagans at home. Sarah is recovering well, but Raymond admits that stones have been thrown by black neighbors also angry about the rumored interracial relationship. So he has decided to sell up and move to Baltimore. Cathy wonders, timidly, spontaneously, if she might one day go to Maryland to visit him: "No one would know us there." But Raymond balks: "What has to matter the most is what's right for Sarah." Cathy is crying by the time he says, "Have a proud life, a splendid life."

She collapses weeping on the bed when she gets home and has to compose herself quickly when Frank phones from a hotel room, which he is sharing with the young man from Miami, to arrange a time to finalize the divorce. Haynes explains in the commentary that the rooms Cathy and Frank occupy were lit so as to totally estrange contrasting hues—blue for Cathy's bedroom, yellow and orange for Frank's hotel—that in earlier scenes had been allowed to mingle. The marriage is finished. Cathy goes to the station and bids a wordless farewell to Raymond before beginning the rest of her life in Hartford.

War of the Worlds

In *Fear Eats the Soul,* Emmi's talk is functional, minimal. A shopkeeper pretends not to know the name of a brand of margarine Ali wants to buy; when she finds out, Emmi reprimands the retailer: "You understand him, all right. But you didn't want to understand. And you know why? Because he's a foreigner! That's why you didn't understand." "No understand 'envious,'" says Ali after the wedding. "Envious is when someone doesn't like a person having something," Emmi explains precisely. She speaks plainly or sometimes not at all. When her neighbors back down from their hostility toward her, Emmi does not refer to the thaw in relations or get into any recrimination; she simply resumes everyday communication with them without fuss. Conversation is not a game for Emmi and Ali. Their directness contrasts starkly with the evasive politeness of *Far from Heaven.* Certainly, rampaging Mona is said by Eleanor to have instigated "talk, vicious talk," but none of this discourse occurs onscreen: Frank's cursing is a rule-proving exception.

Innuendo prevails in Hartford. There are, in particular, the variations played by Cathy's friends on the *Weekly Gazette* characterization of her as "a woman as devoted to her family as she is kind to Negroes." First, Eleanor twists the line ("I'm just delighted to see you taking interest in yet another civic cause. I can see it now: 'Cathleen Whitaker and her kindness to homosexuals'"); then, at the Magnatech party, Dick Dawson (Stevie Ray Dallimore) does too, more provocatively (and flirtatiously): "There are some rather dangerous pro-integration types right here in Hartford. . . . Oh yes, some very attractive ones, in fact, noted, I'm told, for their kindness to Negroes!" Such loaded comments are almost worthy of the devious diplomatic world of *The Earrings of Madame de.* . . .

Cathy and Raymond seem at ease with conversational decorum. They may even be its most accomplished practitioners. Hartford innuendo cloaks malice, while Cathy and Raymond's courtly politeness encodes growing fondness, but the circumlocutory distortion is the same. When Cathy breaks off the friendship, the conversation is formal to the point of sounding stilted, almost archaic. Cathy says: "It isn't plausible for me to be friends with you. You've been so very kind to me, and I've been perfectly reckless and foolish in return." Raymond's response is decorous to the point of including literary language ("Just beyond the fall of grace, behold that ever-shining place"). This language use starts to seem masochistic, like the macho banter in "Homo." Only during their final encounter does Cathy invite Raymond to call her by her first name—which he will never have the opportunity to do again—a far cry from the pleasure Emmi takes in new names: "You know what my name is now? . . . A very long name. Emanuela ben Salem M'Barek Mohammed Mustapha. Sounds terrific, doesn't it?"

Cathy and Raymond know their place, though they do not necessarily know that they know it. While walking in the woods, they muse about belonging and transgression. "Sometimes it's the people outside our world we confide in best," he suggests. She demurs: "But once you do confide, share with someone, they're no longer really outside, are they?" Raymond, however, holds to the notion that the two of them belong to different realms: "There is a world, even here in Hartford, where everybody does indeed look like me. The trouble is, very few people ever leave that world." (During their last conversation, Raymond returns to this topic ruefully: "I've learned my lesson about mixing in other worlds.") The difference between their worldviews is subtle but not fundamental. Raymond's is more pessimistic: he sees the social realm as a collection of enclosed domains that are barely connected to one another—like different blocks of a penitentiary, or like an apartheid system—and the strictness of segregation affords the possibility of kindness among strangers. Cathy's view is more inclusive and hopeful: strangers can become guests and confidants, if permitted. Cathy and Raymond disagree about topography and access arrangements, but they concur that there is no singular, unified social realm in which people can move freely.

Referring in *The Meaning of Sarkozy* to the radical slogan "Another world is possible," the philosopher Alain Badiou qualifies the notion in terms relevant to both *Far from Heaven* and *Fear Eats the Soul*: "We must say this very sentence: 'There is only one world.'" He continues: "The African worker I see in the restaurant kitchen, this Moroccan I see digging a hole in the road, this veiled woman looking after children in a park: all these belong to the same world as me" (60–61). But, Badiou points out, the difficulty is that true equality between people is impossible under capitalism, and so for the time being the one-world declaration is "performative"—a statement of commitment to unity as opposed to "separations, walls, controls, contempt, death, and finally war" (63). The sentence is thus grim testimony to a world so partitioned and mutilated that it may not even deserve the word: "The 'world' of unleashed capitalism and the rich democracies is a false world. Recognizing only the unity of products and monetary signs, it casts the majority of humanity into the devalued world of the 'other,' from which it separates itself by walls and war. In this sense there is not a single world today" (68). When Cathy and Raymond wonder about different worlds, their shared premise is the permanence of environmental mutilation.

Both *Far from Heaven* and *Fear Eats the Soul* explore a form of social cruelty that is not exactly ostracism. The persecution is rather the experience of being surrounded and vilified, space narrowing. Cathy says to Raymond during their walk: "Ever since running into you at the exhibition, I kept wondering what it must be like to be the only one in a room—colored or whatever it was—how that might possibly feel." Later, she talks without much conviction about Baltimore, where the couple could go undercover, fade into the crowd. Seeing no future without walls, contempt, and controls, all she can contemplate is something like the futile fugitive existence of Graves and Nancy in "Horror." In *Fear Eats the Soul,* Emmi is at least more hopeful: "We'll be rich, Ali, and we'll buy ourselves a little piece of heaven." She can even conceive of there being only one world, as opposed to a private heavenly comfort zone—though the notion comes to her only at her most irresolute, and it is desperate in its own way because it is also so lonely: "I'm so happy on the one hand, and on the other I can't bear it anymore. All this hatred! From everyone! Sometimes I wish I were all alone with you in the world, with nobody around us."

Cathy and Raymond look for a safe space halfheartedly, but the walls close in on them. The yard in which their final conversation takes place is so cramped by the dark that they have to rely for light on the odd ember-like radiance emitted by a rose bush.

Place in the Sun

All That Heaven Allows reveals an apparent internal opposition to small-town conformism. Ron takes Cary to a cabin in the woods to attend a party hosted by his friends, Alida (Virginia Grey) and Mick (Charles Drake). Alida explains to Cary that Mick worked in advertising before coming under the influence of guru Ron's self-nurturing philosophy: "I guess all of us are looking for security these days. You see, Mick thought . . . that if he had money and an important position it would make him secure. Then when he met Ron, who didn't have either one and didn't seem to need them, he was completely baffled. The answer was so simple it took Mick a long time to figure it out . . . 'to thine own self be true'—that's Ron. You see Ron's security comes from inside himself, and nothing can ever take it away from him. Ron absolutely refuses to let unimportant things become important, and that's what Mick and I were doing . . . our whole life was devoted to keeping up with the Joneses. But when Mick was wounded and had a lot of time to think, he decided to get off that merry-go-round." Others join the party—a beekeeper with a sideline in painting, someone called Manuel the Lobster King—and Cary is suitably impressed by Ron's jovial singing. This refuge for downsizer self-reliance is a mini-Wrenwood. Cary's children may not like the hunky gardener, and members of the country club may spurn him, but the truth is that he presents no threat to the small-town domain: he just wants to live securely on the outskirts, occasionally swooping in to collect a new disciple. Do Cathy and Raymond come any closer than Cary and Ron to getting out?

"The most beautiful melodramas, like those of Sirk and Ophuls," Haynes wrote in his director's statement, "are the ones that show how the worlds in which these characters live—and the happy endings foisted upon them—are wrong." What is wrong with the world of *Far from Heaven*? It is certainly, and obviously, artificial. Haynes decided to "make locations look like sets," as he explains during the commentary. When Cathy and Frank go to the New Year's Eve party at their Miami hotel ("Celebrate as 1958 Arrives in Our Terrace Restaurant"), the dance floor is lit by a canopy of sheathed lamps; the eerie blue that color-stamps much of the film is a peripheral pale glow. Haynes comments: "Mark [Friedberg] and I wanted to create this beautifully artificial world where the stars were little lights on a drop, and the ocean was conveyed on a flat, with little bits of reflective metallic material in little pieces and little rhinestones that hung off the flat with a fan blowing them underneath to create a shimmer of the ocean." Theatricality is unmissable in the decorated world of *Far from Heaven*. Cathy, upset by Frank's behavior at the Magnatech party, is called by Sybil while confiding in Raymond before they go on the woodland walk. Her line is: "I have to get back." Haynes comments: "I love when she says 'I have to get back,' like she just stepped out of her role—she's in the wings of the theater and she's going back on stage." (Authenticity is deliberately undermined in other areas too. When Raymond talks of the "ever-shining place," Haynes explains during the commentary: "That's an invented quote—perhaps all the dialogue is invented quotes." This recalls the inclusion on the *Velvet Goldmine* sound track of "The Whole Shebang," an ersatz English glam track, rather than a cover version, by the U.S. indie band Grant Lee Buffalo.)

But the commentary stresses cinematographic authenticity too. While Cathy waits for Frank before the appointment with the psychiatrist, the sun suddenly comes out. "I didn't even notice it while we were shooting, and it wasn't until I looked at the dailies on tape," Haynes recalls, that "I saw the sun burst up. It was one of those little miracles that sort of adds to the poignancy of that moment without over-gilding the lily, which was always our delicate balance." At another moment of discomfort, Cathy and Mona are filmed in a Sirk-like low-angle shot (when they talk about "one of those"): "It looks treated," Haynes comments. "It looks like it's been run through some kind of a process, or someone pushed the Technicolor button on the computer, but it's all done naturally. We used gels, we used reflectors, we used some supplementary lighting even in exterior day scenes, but for the most part it's just a magnificent crew." So there is more to the aesthetic of *Far from Heaven* than obvious stylizations, and it is better to emphasize a more or less paradoxical interplay between authenticity and trickery.

Nature and artifice come together in two slightly different uses of costume. First, there are the color-coordinated outfits—red, orange, mossy green—worn by Cathy and her friends for lunch at her place. (It is quite a contrast with the boldly abstract, geometric, and clashing fabrics in *Fear Eats the Soul*.) Dressed like this they form a flock, and the clothing thus connotes peer conformity. The women stand out as a group, like the ladies matchingly dressed for the recital that begins Visconti's *L'innocente* (1976). Second, there is blending of character and scenery. On the woodland walk, Raymond's plaid jacket almost acts as camouflage. Cathy, wearing lilac, stands out in this scene. She has left her group and now presents a rather solitary and out-of-place figure, as Raymond did at the art exhibit. (Raymond does not fit in socially in Hartford, but he refuses to be deterred and tries not to notice disapproving glances that come his way.) There is a stranger variation on camouflage when Eleanor visits the morning after the Magnatech party, wearing a print blouse that resembles the russet-and-gold foliage behind her. The branches she is standing in front of almost appear to be coming out of her garment. This is a very weird look that suggests neither contrast nor resemblance between character and environment, but symbiosis. Just such a relationship is suggested by the commentary's most intriguing statement: Haynes says he wanted to tell "a story that would make you cry because the world itself was unfair, a place where people suffered by no fault of their own"—a "tightly woven" cobweb world of "interdependencies in which one person's tiniest step outside that world would create a chain reaction of struggle and loss." And what may be most disconcerting about the world of *Far from Heaven* is its interactivity rather than its simple artificiality. Hartford could be a video-game-like virtual Sim Town. (Computers are absent from Haynes's films, with the exception of the one that Arthur uses in *Velvet Goldmine* to find Brian's full name.)

The artifice seems to be intelligent. *Far from Heaven* broaches a mutual sensitivity, a strange reciprocity, between inhabitants and environment. Two set-piece scenes are noteworthy. Cathy and Raymond's final conversation begins in a diner that they soon leave because of the other patrons' evident disapproval. Therefore it is out on the street, in front of the cinema, that Cathy tells him their friendship cannot continue. She starts to cry, and as she turns away, he takes her arm, says "Mrs. Whitaker"—and is instantaneously seen and reprimanded by a man across the road, who commands, "You, boy, hands off!" It would resemble an incident at the beginning of *Island of Lost Souls,* Erle C. Kenton's 1933 adaptation of H. G. Wells's *The Island of Doctor Moreau*—as soon as the couple steps beyond the boundary of the rogue medic's encampment they are surrounded, as if they had stepped on a tripwire, by his evolution-accelerated creatures—except that it is thuggish, heavy-handed intimidation that is rendered unnecessary by Hartford's uncanny autoresponsiveness. Like a Venus flytrap, or an immune system, Hartford instantly reacts with minimum force to contain this couple's show of taboo intimacy.

The second scene does not show the environment's disciplinary reflex but something more sympathetic, and stranger still. Cathy waits outside the medical center for Frank, and the sun starts to shine, lighting up her face and the building behind her. There is a cut to lovers kissing on a bench—as if their youthful heterosexual passion were the source of the solar solace, or as though Hartford's weather were briefly giving back to Cathy the Whitakers' vanishing place in the sun that has made her so secure and comfortable until now.

Flower Power

The biopower described by Foucault encourages participation and agreement in order to coerce more effectively. The difference is between education and enforcement, between the gentle manipulations that occur in Stevie's household in *Dottie Gets Spanked* and corporal punishment, as well as the difference between in-person cruelty and impersonal, system-wide power. Perhaps it is also the difference between a crocodile and a sunflower.

A Time to Love and a Time to Die is set on the Nazi home front. Ernst (John Gavin) returns on a furlough to his hometown, where he is reunited with a childhood sweetheart, Elisabeth (Liselotte Pulver). She lives in a shared house presided over by Frau Lieser (Dorothea Wieck). Ernst asks: "Who is that crocodile?" Elisabeth replies: "An official tenant, bombed out of her own place and put here by the authorities. They moved in three more since. . . . I was told I should be happy I'm allowed to have this room for myself. She's a member of the Women's Corps of the Party. I suppose that gives her special rights. She'll probably come back to listen." Frau Lieser aggressively watches their every move, and just when she thinks she has seen enough to denounce them for debauchery ("While I'm in it, this is going to be a decent house—I'm going for the police this instant, and before I return that man had better be out of here and you with it!"), Elisabeth triumphantly shows the wedding certificate that she and Ernst have inveigled from the Nazi bureaucracy. The new husband gloats: "I can see she's delighted, it's written all over her face." There is no subtlety of coercion here, certainly no cooperation. The relationship between the lovers and this apparatchik is one of manifest hostility and antagonism. Threats are out in the open, reactions written all over faces. The agents of the Party that invade Elisabeth's domestic space are identifiably inimical.

There is a home infiltration in *Far from Heaven* too. The morning after the trip to collect Frank from the police station, Cathy is saying a fond goodbye to him as he leaves for work. Right at the moment that they kiss, a flash bulb goes off, and Cathy looks around in alarm. A cut reveals the venerable journalist from the *Weekly Gazette,* Mrs. Leacock (Bette Henritze), and, in front of her, an intent photographer (Jason Franklin). Cathy has forgotten about the interview, and, noticing her momentary consternation, the photographer instantly soothes her: "Pardon me, ma'am." The access-all-areas reporter placates too: "I do apologize, Mrs. Whitaker, but candid views are always the best." Cathy immediately recovers her composure and invites her guests to "make themselves at home." (Mrs. Leacock reappears at the art show. The jolly scribbler hails Cathy in caption form: "Wife of Hartford executive communing with Picasso?!" The photographer is with her again; the two journalists seem inseparable.)

After Frank departs, Cathy sits down for the interview, modestly mentioning that she thinks herself an insufficiently interesting subject to be covered in the paper. Mrs. Leacock shrugs off the notion. "Readers of the *Weekly Gazette,* Mrs. Whitaker, are women just like yourself, with families and homes to keep up. A good society paper need not be a gossip rag. You are the proud wife of a successful sales executive, planning the parties and posing at her husband's side on the advertisements. To everyone here in Connecticut, you are Mr. and Mrs. Magnatech." Just then, Cathy sees Raymond and is initially perturbed by the sight. Says Mrs. Leacock: "Oh my! Mrs Whitaker, perhaps you should call the police." When she summarizes Cathy's social prominence, it is almost as if Mrs. Leacock is on a mission to coaxingly reinforce the socially beneficial identity of Mrs. Magnatech—as if preempting an identified

Apparatus of control (*Far from Heaven*).

danger of disruption. There is also a touch of cold-war indoctrination, in the manner of *The Manchurian Candidate* (dir. John Frankenheimer, 1962), but spoken so congenially by the reassuring, friendly interviewer, never short of a smile or a compliment.

Turned away from the camera, the writer's amusing hat is conspicuous above her grass-stem-green outfit. With its ruglike beige brim, it makes her look like an imitation sunflower—a comic spoof of nature personified, not an instrument of a surveillance machine. After Cathy has reassured herself that Raymond is not dangerous, she comes back inside to pose for her photo. "Isn't that darling," says Mrs. Leacock, and there is a cut to a camera position behind her and the photographer. From that angle, the photographer's ear seems to be part of her body, and his camera appears as an appendage of her fake-floral hat. It is a macabre image of a courteous, coaxing, responsive apparatus of social control in disguise.

Hartford politeness is powerful. "I'm going to the police this instant," says Frau Lieser. What a difference it makes to only have to say instead, as Mrs. Leacock does, "Mrs. Whitaker, perhaps you should call the police"—and, what is more, not to have to call the police at all, because when it matters, Hartford will clamp down automatically, using nothing more violent than a sharp word and the sudden concerted vigilance of passersby. With sunflowers such as this one, there is no need for crocodiles.

Art World

Sirk told Jon Halliday: "I'm not interested in failure in the sense given it by the neo-romantics who advocate the beauty of failure. It is rather the kind of failure that invades you without rhyme or reason"—"an ugly kind of failure, a completely hopeless one . . . there is no exit. All the Euripidean plays have this no exit—there is only one way out, the irony of the 'happy end'" (133, 136). This has a bearing on Cathy's inclusiveness. Her remark that "once you do confide, share with someone, they're no longer really extrior" is preoccupied by the possibilities for accommodation afforded by existing social space. It is an insider opinion, and what is ultimately questioned in *Far from Heaven* is the very existence of an exterior. At the end of the film, there is a "no exit" of nowhere to go. Haynes's tentative title names distant sanctuary, but the film might as well have been called *Nowhere Else,* just as Sirk's *There's Always Tomorrow* amounts to *No Future.*

Far from Heaven begins with a black screen upon which the production credits appear. Then a painting of autumn leaves fades in—not unlike the paintings that begin a cinematic study of duty, unhappiness, and repression by Yasujiro Ozu, such as *An Autumn Afternoon* (1962)—which in turn fades to the reddening leaves of a real tree. Months pass during the narrative course of Haynes's film, and so when the passage from picture to town scene is reversed at the end, there is blossom on the deceptively soothing painted bough on which the cast list is superimposed. If one connotation of the pretty nature picture is springtime rebirth, another is a perimeter construction with nothing beyond it.

The dauber at the self-help cabin party in *All that Heaven Allows* declares (in keeping with the smug occasion): "I'm not an abstractionist—strictly primitive." There is an even better modern-art joke in Sirk's comedy, *Has Anybody Seen My Gal* (1952). A millionaire in disguise, Samuel (Charles Coburn), pretends to be a painter and shows off a hand-smeared abstract to a little girl (with whom he is also singing a musical number) with the comment: "That is sur-real-ism. Sur-real-ism: that's a new school of painting founded in Paris. Instead of painting what you see, you paint what you feel inside of you. At least that's what they say it means." The extra irony of this modern-art parodying is that the scene unmistakably occurs in a studio with a painted backdrop. There is a similar sleight of hand in the final voiceover Haynes wrote for *Far from Heaven* but decided not to use: "That was the day I stopped believing in the wild ardor of things. Perhaps in love, as well," Cathy says. "The love in books and films. The love that tells us to abandon our lives and plans, all for one brief touch of Venus. . . . So often we fail in that kind of love. The world just seems too fragile a place for it. Or perhaps it's only we who are too fragile." It is comforting self-deception. The Hartford world is really not fragile at all: it is socially regimented and auto-regulating, though it keeps outright punishment to a minimum. Cathy's reference to "books and films" involves the same irony as Samuel's talk of Parisian innovation. When she invokes fiction, she makes the distinction between artwork and world that actually fails in *Far from Heaven*.

Hartford is much worse than Van Gogh's nursery. At least the caged bird can see the busy domain outside the bars; at least there is somewhere to escape to should the opportunity arise. The prisoner has what Hannibal Lecter (Anthony Hopkins), confined to a subterranean cell in *The Silence of the Lambs* (dir. Jonathan Demme, 1991), yearns for: a view. In another letter to his brother, dated October 22, 1882, quoted by Artaud in "The Man Suicided by Society," Van Gogh developed the idea of capture more bleakly in terms of solitary confinement, but still compensated by associating art making with prison breaking. "What is drawing? How does one come to it? It is working through an invisible iron wall that seems to stand between what one *feels* and what one *can do.* How is one to get through that wall—since pounding at it is of no use? In my opinion one has to undermine that wall, filing through it steadily and patiently" (206). The backdrop logic of *Far from Heaven* does not even permit acknowledgment of this dungeon three-dimensionality, with its invisible but accessible beyond. An outside is unthinkable.

The surrealist painting in *Far from Heaven,* Miró's *The Nightingale's Song at Midnight and the Morning Rain,* greatly interests Cathy and Raymond. They discuss it sensitively at the Hartford Cultural Center. Haynes cuts from their earnest peering faces to a pan across the picture that discovers the odd horned bird on the right side of the canvas. The creature blends in: it is as much ground as figure. Though it is alert and seems to be checking up on other semi-beings above it, existing in only one dimension means its gaze cannot extend beyond the immediate environs. This weird flat world is the only home it has. Call that strange stuck creature Cathy.

I'm Not There

Keeping Up with the Joneses

Somewhat like *Velvet Goldmine*, *I'm Not There* invitingly creates an intricate dream realm filled with songs and allusions, a Dylanological Tardis for the maverick star's fictional regeneration in parallel universes. "The film is confusing," Greil Marcus wrote in *Bob Dylan by Greil Marcus*, "only if one demands that a dream explain itself" (375). But roam around a while, and this domain of the Dylanesque comes to seem paradoxical, troubling, hemmed in—a "Lost Land," to quote one of the chapter titles of the singer's 2004 memoir, *Chronicles*—and it even starts to make a freakish kind of sense.

After a motorcycle crash on a long, straight country road, Jude Quinn (Cate Blanchett) lies on a mortuary trolley, dead in the offscreen crash. "A devouring public can now share the remains of his sickness," intones Kris Kristofferson's suavely low-voiced narrator as a scalpel cuts into the corpse. "There he lay: poet, prophet, outlaw, fake, star of electricity, nailed by a Peeping Tom who would soon discover . . . even the ghost was more than one person." The narrator's statement is derived from Dylan's own freeform novel, *Tarantula*: "here lies bob dylan / demolished by Vienna politeness— / which will now claim to have invented him / the cool people can / now write Fugues about him / & Cupid can now kick over his kerosene lamp— / bob dylan—killed by a discarded Oedipus / who / turned around / to investigate a ghost / & discovered that / the ghost too / was more than one person" (102). So much attention has been paid to the plurality of Dylans in *I'm Not There* that something mentioned by Dylan that the characters mostly have in common can be overlooked: coolness.

Alongside Jude are Woody (Marcus Carl Franklin), the fake, a black boy with a guitar who is on a hobo journey through a verdant alternative America that is home also to the outlaw, Billy (Richard Gere), hiding in Missouri; Jack Rollins (Christian Bale), the prophet, a protest singer who becomes a Pentecostal pastor in Stockton, California; Arthur (Ben

Whishaw), the poet who sullenly gives gnomic evidence at a tribunal; and Robbie Clarke (Heath Ledger), an iconic movie actor famed for his performances in the *Every Grain of Sand* and *Gang Plank*, the star of electricity and husband of the abstract painter Claire Montfort Clark (Charlotte Gainsbourg).

The widely praised Jude section conjures with two chic manifestations of 1960s monochrome cinema: Fellini-esque European art cinema and the U.S. vérité documentary pioneered by D. A. Pennebaker and his ilk. The Jude scenes morph the 1965–66 period when Dylan became not just a folk star but a mainstream pop star, a breakout that caused consternation among devotees of one-man-and-his-acoustic-guitar topical songs. Dylan famously decided to go electric, recording the *Highway 61 Revisited* album that includes "Like a Rolling Stone," and animosity toward his new sound distilled into the cry of "Judas!" that came from the audience during the gig he played with his backing group, the Hawks (later the Band), at the Manchester Free Trade Hall in May 1966.

The black-and-white poise of the re-created tour in *I'm Not There* softens the actual color footage of these 1966 performances, shot by Pennebaker for the unreleased film *Eat the Document* and excerpted in Martin Scorsese's *No Direction Home: Bob Dylan* (2005). When I reviewed this documentary for *Sight and Sound,* I was struck most of all by an impression that Dylan seems under major stress, jolted by the power of the band's music, as if he had not simply picked up a Stratocaster but actually plugged himself into the mains—for example, performing "Like a Rolling Stone" in Newcastle: "Rickety-seeming and stick thin in a tight black velvet suit, Dylan looks like a high-heeled marionette. At his left, guitarist Robbie Robertson watches with an expression veering between concern and euphoria; he stands like a bodyguard while Dylan is convulsed by the song, which he shouts out—at one point cupping his hands around his mouth as if the better to let the words pour out of him, his exhausted eyes directed way over the heads of the audience, his face jerking skittishly as if he were being administered electric shocks" (92). But there is none of this in *I'm Not There*'s rendition of the Manchester concert. Svelte in houndstooth, Jude is lounge-lizard smooth. Blanchett's game-faced performance is as much interpretation as impersonation: Dylan as hipster. Near the end of the film, Jude says, "Everybody knows

I'm not a folk singer," and then smiles—serenely, smugly, with a camera-loves-me complacency that takes the audience's approval for granted in a way that pop-star Dylan in 1966 never did.

Earlier, during a party scene, Jude is introduced to Brian Jones (Matthew Boylan), the drummer for the Rolling Stones, and the singer puts down the English muso by referring to the Stones as "that groovy covers band." Yet it is the immaculate Jude scenes that have the traits of a high-production-values cover version that for the most part overconfidently misfires, apart from some devilish details. The best moments in this section of *I'm Not There* involve another Jones, Keenan (Bruce Greenwood), the predatory TV pundit for *Culture Beat*, based on the Mr. Jones character in Dylan's *Highway 61 Revisited* song "Ballad of a Thin Man." This spiteful critic loses no opportunity to rankle or harangue Jude, and digs up the singer's past with the zeal of a two-bit Torquemada. In a happily unhinged scene, it is Keenan who splits into several persons in a restroom, with one incarnation stark naked. And, according to the same rule of beneficial sidetracking, the second best thing about the Jude section is the interlude in which the Black Panther Party for Self-Defense cofounder Bobby Seale (Benz Antoine), in the middle of a massage, tells his cohort Huey P. Newton (Craig Thomas) to play "Ballad of a Thin Man" again so he can figure out the song's politics.

The Jude section does not acknowledge it, but there is an uncool Dylan. At one point in *Don't Look Back* (1967), Pennebaker's black-and-white documentary about the 1965 U.K. tour, Dylan remonstrates with the entourage in his hotel suite because someone has thrown a glass out the window. His outburst is most un-rock-star-like, more befitting a newly anointed hall monitor. He demands that whoever threw the object admit the deed to hotel management: "I wanna know who threw that glass in the street. . . . Who did it? Now you better tell me—if someone don't tell me who did it, you're all gonna get the fuck out of here and never come back. Now who did it? I don't care who did it, man, I just wanna know who did it." There is a similar oddball dutifulness in Dylan's bit part as Alias in Sam Peckinpah's *Pat Garrett and Billy the Kid* (1973), and this quality only comes through in *I'm Not There* in the scenes with Jack, once he has become the straggly bearded, sallow, haggard pastor of Gateway Brotherhood church. He is the least glamorous and beautiful of the pseudo-Dylans, and the most thorny, a spokesman for a reactionary evangelism: "And we here in America, we shall overcome. What greater honor for a nation than to speak for God? Some say that the war to end all wars has already begun right now in the Middle East. For it is prophesied that the weak will fall and that Jesus will set up his kingdom in Jerusalem, so why should we worry?"

Rimbaud Returns

I'm Not There revisits the Haynes archive as well as the Dylan back catalog, but there is something jaded in the return. References to previous Haynes films occur in the casting of Bale, Julianne Moore as Alice Fabian (a Joan Baez–like character who appears in the Rollins mock-documentary), and Peter Friedman (the charlatan Peter Dunning in *Safe*) in two cameo roles (Morris Bernstein in the Rollins profile, and the Barker in the Riddle sequence of Billy's story). The most substantial revisitation comes in the brief Arthur scenes. Some kind of grand jury has been convened to probe this mercurial, tousle-haired scribbler who spells out his surname as he begins his deposition—"R-I-M-B-A-U-D"—and then asks, "What's all this about?" When the questions come, they are more playful than forensic in this safe-seeming courtroom, and Arthur even smokes a cigarette as he filibusters—calling himself a farmer, then a trapeze artist—and denies being fatalistic. He speaks about his creative process—"It was like swimming in lava, skipping, kicking, catching a nail with your foot, seeing your victim hanging from a tree"—and makes other gnomic, absurdist, or symbolist remarks. On one of his last appearances, a morose Arthur pronounces: "Never create anything. It will be misinterpreted. It will chain you and follow you for the rest of your life. It will never change."

Haynes here refashions his graduation film, *Assassins*, a forty-minute work in eight numbered segments with mostly pseudoscientific or alchemical titles: "Calcination," "Putrefaction," "Solution," "Distillation," "Sublimation," "Conjunction," "Fixation," and "(return to start)." The depiction in *Assassins* of a pair of rebellious and scandalous artists, Rimbaud (Bruce Cree) and Paul Verlaine (Phelim Dolan), anticipates *Velvet Goldmine,* while a secondary focus on Paul's cheated-on wife Mathilde (Mellissa Brown) anticipates *Far from Heaven. Assassins* has a precocious, proto–New Queer bravado in one particularly striking shot. "Sublimation" begins with a sudden return to the present: a young man who resembles Haynes himself is typing in a bright room, while a dark-haired companion leans intimately over his shoulder. They look around, and the camera begins a shaky room-film tour that encompasses someone's hands apparently emerging from a chest (as if playing a joke with Hitchcock's 1948 *Rope*) and ends with the sight, reflected from somewhere else in a metafictional magic mirror like the one in *Beauty and the Beast,* of two men having sex.

In several abject images, Arthur is collapsed or dying. One ingenious flourish begins with Paul wandering along an old wooden jetty before the lofty camera leaves him behind as it tilts down along the weathered planks to discover Arthur recumbent on the jetty's coffin-like lower platform. The dead-poet pathos of *Assassins* is supplemented by exuberance at other times and, at the end, by enigmatic restraint. The final shot is a movie portrait, accompanied by mournful choral singing mixed with whispers and then spoken fragments of quotation, finishing with Haynes saying the last line of Rimbaud's "Morning of Drunkenness": "Now is the time of the Assassins." For ninety seconds, Cree dressed as Arthur looks to camera. It is a take on Andy Warhol's mid-1960s *Screen Tests* (some of which are available on the DVD *Thirteen Most Beautiful: Songs for Andy Warhol's Screen Tests*). Cree's closeup is most like Edie Sedgwick's: sexy, a little sleepy, at once accessible and unapproachable—possessed of a reticent cool more intriguing than Jude's aplomb. (Michelle Williams's character in *I'm Not There,* Coco Rivington, who flirts with Jude, is partly based on Sedgwick.) The sourness of the 2007 Arthur is pronounced when

A jaded poet (*I'm Not There*).

Screen test
(*Assassins*).

contrasted with this 1985 portrait, which is a pity, given that Whishaw's Arthur is the closest *I'm Not There* comes to a gay Dylan.

Parenthood

Claire wakes up with a slightly distressed look on her face. She chats with her two daughters as she pours milk over cereal. The TV news is on while she tidies up later, and when she hears Nixon announcing that an agreement has been signed to deliver "peace with honor in Vietnam," she freezes, and Robbie's murmured voiceover is heard: "That's when she knew it was over for good. The longest-running war in television history, the war that hung like a shadow over the same nine years of her marriage. So why was it suddenly so hard to breathe?" (Claire gets a voiceover of her own later.) Less politically momentous news follows: a report that Robbie and his *Gang Plank* costar are romantically linked. The neglected wife ponders her earth-colored abstract paintings hanging on the wall and then leafs through an exhibition catalog for her *Recent Works* show before seeing a clip of Thích Quảng Đức's 1963 self-immolation on the TV. In a flashback to 1964, Claire is studying at Cooper Union when she has a date with Robbie in a diner. They fall in love. She rides pillion on his motorbike and translates Rimbaud's famous I'm-not-there letter for him: "I is someone else. I am present at the birth of my thought: I watch and I listen."

Back in the time of the separation, she collects the girls from their caretaker in a park. The scene is idyllic: Claire wraps them both up in a hug, the camera lazily zooming in. Then there is a cut to closer shots of the trio rolling around on the grass, perfectly relaxed. The accompanying Dylan track is a strange choice. "Simple Twist of Fate" is a breakup song about a fretful man reflecting on lost love in a hotel: "He woke up, the room was bare / He didn't see her anywhere." It appears on the 1974 album *Blood on the Tracks,* which Mike Marqusee characterized in *Chimes of Freedom*: "The contradictions, the double standards, are all expressions of a boy-man lost in a world of temptations and frustrations, torn between the thirst for autonomy and the siren song of complete surrender" (182). This describes feckless, promiscuous Robbie well enough, but at this point in *I'm Not There,* the glaring contradiction is between the dismayed song and the sentimentality of this parent-and-kids episode. There are three figures onscreen, but the family group is mush and mess compared to the rigid, frightening, out-of-line family images that appear in other Haynes films. Perhaps the only interesting way to resolve the contradictions between sound and image, and between this scene and others in Haynes's work, is to interpret the mawkishness as Robbie's hypocritical idealization.

The rifts in the marriage are exposed during a lunch with friends. Bad-tempered Robbie offends everyone when he says that "chicks can never be poets." Claire cannot contain her indignation: "Robbie, please, you're not serious. . . . I cannot believe you're actually saying these things. . . . I want to know what this thing is that women cannot experience . . . or write about or talk about or put on paper. . . . What is this place? Do you own this place? Did you invent it?" Later they sit in separate rooms of their beach house. The end is near, but before it arrives, Robbie and Claire have unconvincingly tender and laid-back sex, "Idiot Wind" on the sound track (not the *Blood on the Tracks* version but the sketchier, slower recording from *The Bootleg Series 1961–1991*). Again the song is a mismatch, especially given that the sex scene looks like newfound desire, not defunct love. Plaintive the melody of "Idiot Wind" may be, but the words are more tantrum than tantric: "You're an idiot, babe / It's a wonder that you still know how to breathe." Further ill-fitting images follow: a closeup of the girls' glitter-encrusted paintings and, after a shot of a displeased Robbie exiting the divorce court, a high-angle shot of

Claire meeting the girls in the parking lot outside. It is filmed from inside the courthouse, the view impeded by a metal grille, and it epitomizes the volte-face that much of *I'm Not There* undertakes: this is an institutional view separate from, but wholly appropriate to, the celebrity marriage pangs that are insider tribulations out of kilter with the usual concerns of Haynes's films. (This rupture of an artist couple has none of the hurt that comes when Mandy and Brian go their separate and childless ways in *Velvet Goldmine*.) It is true that Dylan repeatedly made clear his own commitment to family life in *Chronicles*, but as songs like "Idiot Wind" and "I'm Not There" (which also plays during the Claire-and-Robbie section) testify, not at the expense of a more dire dimension of experience: "As long as my own form of certainty stayed intact, I owed nobody nothing. I wasn't going to go deeper into the darkness for anybody. I was already living in the darkness. My family was my light, and I was going to protect that light at all cost. This is where my dedication was, first, last, and everything in-between. What did I owe the rest of the world? Nothing. Not a damn thing" (123).

The darkness that is also so characteristic of Haynes's work is hard to find in *I'm Not There*. The film's about-turn can be measured in regard to two scenes involving Claire that replay moments from earlier films. First Claire, alone, looks at her exhibition catalog. She is surrounded by her outsized abstract paintings that loom on the walls like craters. The artwork ambience continues with a dim, blue-black montage that begins with an allusion to the statue shots in Jean-Luc Godard's *Contempt* (1963), as the camera circles around an ancient figure of a woman; moves to a nighttime, slightly sinister closeup of Robbie on the move; and then concludes with a shadowy view of a reproduction of the *Mona Lisa* before Claire closes the catalog. The multimedia darkness here is decorative, and it fails to add up to anything more than a sort of mood board. The outsized art, a female artist's unhappy introspection, and the grisly 1960s found footage (which will subsequently include Watergate-era clips of Nixon and Vietnam) all invite comparison with *Superstar*—only without the torment or encroaching menace.

Second is when Claire wakes up dazed and then gets breakfast for the girls. The sequence closely resembles the scene in *Safe* that concludes with Carol drinking milk with uncanny absent-mindedness. In *I'm Not There*, Claire blithely sets her relationship troubles aside while she serves soccer-mom bowls of cereal—Dylan recalled less healthy family food in *Chronicles*: "hot dogs with English muffins and noodles, the Cheerios and cornflakes with heavy cream" (125)—and chatters about a forthcoming boat trip. The scene is a straight-faced portrayal of what was referred to ironically in one of the mock-documentary sequences in *Superstar*: "Few could leave the supermarket without buying more than they intended and the kitchen, often the center of the home, contained an ever-expanding variety of foods. Home life in America connoted the cozy kitchen, food preparation, and mealtime." Claire may be unhappy, but her creativity and confident parenthood make her safe. Self-help commitment is the hallmark when she takes over the voiceover (in a late shot of her sitting at a writing desk). It would please another Claire, Wrenwood's director in *Safe,* for it ends with rejoice: "Because relations are always ambiguous and I continue to fail to communicate, because I continue to blame myself even when I'm not to blame, because each failing has made me more remote from myself, from my babies, and from you"—there is a cut to an image of her speaking to camera—"for all these reasons and many more still unknown, I must listen, I must look around more than ever, I must live."

Americana

Haynes's decision to cast a black actor as a version of Dylan is anticipated in *Chronicles*: "I wondered if Denzel [Washington] could play Woody Guthrie. In my dimension of reality, he certainly could have" (187). But what kind of dimension is it that *I'm Not There*'s Woody shares with Billy (who finds the young troubadour's guitar on a train at the end of the film)? Is it, for example, what Dylan elsewhere in his memoir called (acknowledging Marcus's *Invisible Republic,* otherwise known as *The Old, Weird America*) "some different republic, some liberated republic" (34) such as folk songs reveal?

It is 1959: Woody, guitar case slung on his back, is running across a verdant pasture as a locomotive cuts through the countryside. He hops into a car and settles down for the ride, falling into conversation about his musical influences with two hobos. He spins tales about a wandering life that appears in flashback: a muddy carnival where he is jeered, a porch where he plays guitar with two men (one of whom is the musician Richie Havens). Three drifters try to steal his guitar, and he jumps out of the train as it passes over a river bridge. In the water he enters a black-and-white fable, filmed like the pub hallucination in Carol Reed's *Odd Man Out* (1947). After a whale gobbles up the youth and swims away from camera, a hand suddenly appears before a reverse shot shows Claire with her hand pressed against glass. Woody wakes up in the hospital and then stays with the couple who found him after his plunge. But after a phone call comes from a Minnesota juvenile center with an inquiry about a young fugitive, he hits the road again, making his way by bus to visit the dying Guthrie at a New Jersey hospital. There are hospital or clinic scenes in most of Haynes's films, some of which—Carol being wheeled on the gurney in *Safe*, the death of Ray (Quinn McColgan) in *Mildred Pierce*—are horrible and painful. By far the most benign and welcoming infirmary is this pre–civil rights one in *I'm Not There*, where, just after Dylan sings (again jarringly) about "the ghosts of slavery ships" on the accompanying "Blind Willie McTell," young black Woody is directed without suspicion to room 300 to sit at his hero's bedside. As with Claire's kitchen, an institutional space that seems oppressive in other Haynes films is safe in *I'm Not There*.

In another part of this curiously pacified country, Billy is hiding out in the woods beyond the town of Riddle, Missouri. His friend Homer (Paul J. Spence) tells him that Commissioner Pat Garrett (Bruce Greenwood—another double role) has successfully pushed through a plan to develop the Shadow Valley area and build a highway through the town. Riddle is circusville, its inhabitants masked and costumed as Billy wanders past. The populace includes, according to Haynes's commentary, "a boy pirate, a girl hunchback of Notre Dame, a boy prince, a teenage Houdini in chains, a little boy Teddy Roosevelt, a Lincoln on stilts, a small girl dressed as a tumbleweed, a gangly teen joker, an Ophelia girl strewn in river weed, a girl Mary Pickford, a boy Mr. Peanut, and a series of ghost and goblin masks inspired by the photographer Ralph Eugene Meatyard." On an old bandstand, Jim James of the band My Morning Jacket in whiteface sings "Goin' to Acapulco." Billy pats his horse while he listens and says in voiceover: "Trouble was, I'd grown partial to the place—that sudden smell of fear, and the thrill of waiting up for the end of the world." It is dark, apocalyptic talk. In keeping with it, the scene slowly fades to black and then cuts, shockingly, to an overhead black-and-white shot of a tarantula (inspired by an image in the opening montage of *Persona*) that introduces a party in the Jude section.

The "sudden smell of fear" is little more than talk. A newspaper headline hypes the onetime "FAMED CAPTOR OF OUTLAW BILLY THE KID," but the lawman is past his prime, if indeed he is an enforcer at all anymore, as opposed to a geriatric bureaucrat who reassures the townsfolk about an "evacuation fund" having been established for "eligible evacuees." Billy, calling himself William, challenges Garrett (who almost recognizes him), "Why are you going through our town?" For a moment it seems like Billy will stir up a revolt, but then a bowler-hatted bailiff on the stand quells the commotion and has the agitator taken away. In a scene reminiscent of the limo drive in *The Man Who Fell to Earth* (dir. Nicolas Roeg, 1976), Billy is driven to jail, passing Homer standing at the roadside on the way. The outlaw is locked up once more, but that night he removes the cell bars with a hammer and chisel, then heads for the railroad at dawn. Haynes says during the commentary: "I knew Billy had to be thrust back into the world. So, in escaping his exile, he's forced back onto the train . . . into locomotion, back onto the Never Ending Tour where Dylan resides today." It is the simplest escape in all of Haynes's films; the prison bars come away with ease, recalling the words of the traditional song, "Big Rock Candy Mountain": "In the Big Rock Candy Mountains the jails are made of tin / And you can walk right out again as soon as you are in." It is too good to be true. This misery-free, pastoral, green-and-gold Missouri, with its dotard Garrett, is more quarantine zone than frontier territory. If it has any parallel in Haynes's work, it is the false refuge of Baton in "Homo."

In the animated *Watership Down* (dir. Martin Rosen, 1978), rabbits flee their repressive colony through farmland. During a rainstorm they meet an ingratiating rabbit called Cowslip, who languidly invites them to shelter in one of the empty burrows in his warren. Underground, the intuitive Fiver grows increasingly alarmed at their spacious new surroundings. There is an abundance of food there, but Fiver is too distressed to eat: "There's something unnatural and evil and twisted about this place. It feels—it feels like mist, like being deceived and losing our way." These words also fit the Woody and Billy sections of *I'm Not There.*

Citizenship

It could be said that Billy has scurried like a spider into a hiding place—a description suggested by a scene in the Jude section in which Allen Ginsberg (David Cross) reads from the "Of the Tarantulas" chapter in Friedrich Nietzsche's *Thus Spoke Zarathustra*, which also contains this proposition: "That they speak well of life, these poison spiders, although they sit in their caves and with their backs turned on life, is because they want to do harm by speaking well of life" (124). Though it has a measure of heartache, *I'm Not There*'s account of life is, by the standard of Haynes's films, exceptionally benign. It speaks well of life, but at the periphery, fright and nightmare stalk it.

I discovered Greil Marcus's book *Invisible Republic: The World of Bob Dylan's Basement Tapes* in the summer of 2000. When I finished reading it, I turned back to the beginning and retraced the path toward the "City on a Hill" chapter, in which Marcus discusses "Tears of Rage" and "I'm Not There" as songs about national community in crisis: "the song asks if America even exists" (204), said Marcus about the second of these laments. I listened to both songs repeatedly, day after day. At a certain point, "Tears of Rage" fell away, and I was left with "I'm Not There."

In *No Direction Home,* Dylan recalls the impact of Johnny Ray in words that apply to the way Dylan himself sings "I'm Not There": "He had some kind of strange incantation in his voice like he'd been voodooed, and he cried kinda when he sang." "I'm Not There" sounds as if all a haunted country's anguish could find expression in it, only to grow more grief-struck as the track proceeds. "The mood grows more awful as the song moves on," Marcus wrote. "In the last lines of the song, the most plainly sung, the most painful, so bereft that after the song's five minutes, five minutes that seem like no measurable time, you no longer quite believe that anything so strong *can* be said in words" (193–94). It still sends shivers down my spine, and so does Marcus's writing that unlocked it for me. *I'm Not There* must have unlocked it for many others, for this basement recording, made in late 1967 or early 1968, and known also as "I'm Not There (1956)," was released officially for the first time on the soundtrack album for Haynes's film.

Marcus reissued the book in 2011 under the title he had originally intended, *The Old, Weird America,* with a new preface that mentions

I'm Not There as being "named for the most distant and alluring of the basement tapes songs" (xiii). Lately both the allure and the distance of the song have started to trouble me. "I'm Not There" tells of a woman who "cries both day and night" and whom the singer claims to be able to comfort. When he is with her she is content, but now she is "forsaken," abandoned. He has left her, or she has been hauled away, and the song moves from her suffering to his, from her endless weeping to his regret, with which the song ends: "I wish I was there to help her but I'm not there, I'm gone." Can her sorrow and his coexist in "I'm Not There," or does his leave hers behind once he takes over as the dirge's subject? What has happened to her during its course, and whose side is the song on? According to Marcus: "The town has already abandoned her; by common will or her own, she is already outside of society, ostracized, banished, a self-made mute, a hermit—the cause can't be known, but her fate can't be questioned. The singer sings with such mortification because he knows the only way he can reach this woman is to place himself outside of society" (194). Indications are that the singer prefers to be an insider, and if so, his grief would be a sentiment expressed in social safety and—which may be Marcus's point—at the cost of assent to scapegoating, whether symbolic or not. (Read like this, "I'm Not There" would be on the other side of experience than the so-lonely "Superstar.") The "I" of "I'm Not There" would assert itself over the duration of the song in the name of the social obedience occasionally broached in *Chronicles*, as in a gloss on the strategist Clausewitz: "When he claims that politics has taken the place of morality and politics is brute force, he's not playing. You have to believe it. You do exactly as you're told, whoever you are. Knuckle under or you're dead. Don't give me any of that jazz about hope or nonsense about righteousness" (45).

I have wondered about the politics of Haynes's films in similar terms because of the struggle that persistently plays out in them between cruel social norms and carnivalesque alternatives, dungeon worlds and more or less untrustworthy sanctuaries. But when I follow this train of thought, it always leads me to conclude that his films are not underpinned by any true belonging. If they were, the nightmarish perception of entrapment would not be so recurring and resilient—even in *I'm Not There*, which tamps down the misery.

Dylan wrote in *Chronicles* about the sorrowfulness of his songs in terms of bad vision: "I really was never any more than what I was—a folk musician who gazed into the gray mist with tear-blinded eyes and made up songs that floated in a luminous haze" (116). The impairment is actually triple: mist, tears, haze. But the horror that sometimes emerges in *I'm Not There* is more conducive to a clear view. It is the idea of a partitioned panopticon world encased in glass.

Heading for Riddle, Billy rides out from the cabin on a breezy morning, stopping to contemplate a huge forest. As he looks toward the horizon, Eddie Vedder and the Million Dollar Bashers' cover of "All Along the Watchtower" fades in, and there is an unexpected cut to archival footage of Indochina conflagrations. The editing makes it seem like the explosions are in Billy's line of vision before the sequence takes another surprise turn: a zoom-out that reveals these phantom war images appearing on Claire's TV set. The editing means that the TV screen intervenes like a window between Billy and Claire. Then, after Billy is rebuked from the bandstand, there is a cut to Keenan sitting in the back seat of a car as the window rolls up. He looks toward camera, as if he too were peering into Billy's world. And this is exactly what Claire does when she suddenly appears at the other side of an aquarium wall, dream witness through glass to Woody being swallowed by the cetacean. When *I'm Not There* returns to Missouri after the brief interlude with Keenan, by which time "I'm Not There" has started up on the sound track, Billy is himself inside a car—which actually seems out of place in this Western-like story—and then there is a match cut to him standing in the ineffective prison. The bars on which he places his hands are the obvious markers of imprisonment, but the glimpses of separating glass are images of a more effective and total containment.

I'm Not There cuts from the Missouri jailhouse back to black-and-white London, and it is in cool Jude's section that the world-behind-glass anxiety of being an insider is most plainly depicted. Tired and wasted, Jude sits down at the celebrity party. Tom Verlaine and the Million Dollar Bashers' cover of "Cold Irons Bound" plays. (This is an anachronistic song, since it appears on the 1997 *Time Out of Mind* album, but its theme of captivity is fitting: "I'm twenty miles out of town in cold irons bound.") The surrounding white-cube walls suddenly become screens on which appears the face of Lyndon B. Johnson. By the scale of this presidential

On the inside (*I'm Not There*).

visage, which looms like the Partridge Family clip in *Superstar*, Jude is tiny, an insect that might be a juicy morsel for the tarantula glimpsed earlier, which now slowly walks on the other side of the translucent partition that the walls have become.

I'm Not There speaks well of life; the suspicion of family and other institutions that permeates Haynes's films startlingly gets eclipsed. But when windows open up between seemingly liberated dimensions, or a gigantic spider looms over the good life, the film's eclectic ecosystem reveals itself as a climate-controlled vivarium. Billy could perform his Houdini act in every jailhouse in the land and still never get out of the ant farm.

Mildred Pierce

Identification of a Woman

There is a slapstick incident in James M. Cain's novel *Mildred Pierce*, which understandably makes no appearance in either Michael Curtiz's 1945 Hollywood adaptation or Haynes's more faithful HBO miniseries. Mildred and Bert are arguing about their divorce, and he needles her. She turns the tables in an unexpected fashion: "In his palmiest days as a picture extra, Bert never did such a take'm as he did at that moment, with the dough doing service as a pie. It caught him square in the face, hung there for a moment, and parted to reveal tragic, uninjured dignity. . . . He said she ought to know by now she couldn't pull the wool over his eyes. Then he had to go to the sink to wash his face, and while he clawed the dough away, she talked" (90). It is a comic moment but with a disturbing edge: Bert is made faceless, pulpy, by being covered in cake mix. The incident is more uncanny than it seems at first, and the same can be said of the miniseries.

To a large extent, Haynes's adaptation undoes Curtiz's noir reworking. Gone is the added police-interrogation frame story involving the murder of Mildred's husband, Monte (not Monty) Beragon (Zachary Scott), which turns out to have been committed by her vampish daughter, Veda (Ann Blyth). Curtiz's crime-film spin involves a process of elimination that leads to Veda being found out. Inspector Peterson (Moroni Olsen), in charge of the inquiry, stage-manages its denouement. He gives a speech timed to end just as the office door opens to reveal the culprit, who has been apprehended at the airport: "See, Mrs. Beragon, we've had a slant on you from the beginning. You were the key, and we had to put the pressure on you. Well, the key turned, the door opened, and there was the murderer." Mildred continues to lie for her daughter, but the whodunit identification cannot be stopped.

However, noir is not simply abandoned in Haynes's *Mildred Pierce*: neo-noir sneaks in by the back door because the miniseries' cinematography and production design are modeled on the look of 1970s New Hollywood: Alan J. Pakula's *Klute* and *The Parallax View* (1974), Francis Ford Coppola's *The Godfather* (1972), Robert Altman's *McCabe and Mrs. Miller* (1971) and *Nashville* (1975), Roman Polanski's *Chinatown* (1974), and even William Friedkin's *The Exorcist* (1973). Accordingly, the miniseries' restricted lighting is naturalistic, and closeups are avoided. The director of photography, Ed Lachman, commented on the *Mildred Pierce* Web site: "With Mildred, we tried to create a certain distance, as if she's being observed. So there's always something between her and us."

Yet the under-surveillance mise-en-scène that conveys vigilance also impairs visibility. In part 4 of the miniseries, in a scene that departs from the novel, Mildred turns private investigator after eighteen-year-old Veda (Evan Rachel Wood) leaves home under a cloud. She parks her car outside her daughter's new apartment to try to catch a glimpse. There is a cut to an image of upstairs windows: the person who closes the thin drapes is Veda, but she is a silhouette, a dark shape, recognizable only because of her distinctive hat and hairstyle. She moves from one window to the other, then pauses before drawing the second set of curtains to block even this meager view. Mildred looks flustered as she drives away: what she has seen was not worth seeing and, if the murky figure's pause means anything, she was countersurveilled by Veda in the process. It is a far cry from a similar nighttime L.A. scene in *Chinatown* when Jake (Jack Nicholson) tracks Evelyn (Faye Dunaway) to a house in the suburbs. The gumshoe creeps around the side of the building and looks through the open curtains to spy the woman's supposedly missing daughter inside. The camera zooms in to emphasize both the surreptitious looking and the fact that an awful truth has come to light. Cries Evelyn in agony afterwards, manifesting both her maternal love and the magnitude of her filial trauma: "She's my sister *and* my daughter. . . . My father and I—understand?" The incest revelation epitomizes the noir world of family secrets that Haynes's *Mildred Pierce* hollows out.

Veda, a gifted sight-reader of music, is a better sleuth than her doting mother. At the end of part 1, Mildred shares her doubts about working as a waitress with her neighbor, Lucy Gessler (Melissa Leo). The friendly encounter takes a creepy turn once the conversation finishes. The women walk into the next room, but the camera hangs back and then turns around, past the evening shadows on the wall, somber bassoon notes marking its arrival at a window fronted with an iron railing. Redheaded, eleven-year-old Veda (Morgan Turner) is standing quietly outside, having eavesdropped. Like the later apartment scene, though,

Rear window (*Mildred Pierce*).

there is an element of unreadability that complicates the private investigation. The girl's back is turned, and her reaction to what she has heard is no more evident than if her face had been covered in batter.

Family Business

Jazz is playing on the sound track while Mildred bakes exquisite pies and then frosts a huge, made-to-order chocolate cake. It is 1931 in Glendale, California, a time of economic hardship. Bert tells Mildred that he is stepping out. "If you go out that door"—in order to visit the residence of one Mrs. Maggie Biederhof—"I swear to God, Bert, I'm not letting you back inside." Mildred is true to her word, which is why, the next day, she goes to an employment agency. Lucy (a smalltime bootlegger) sums up the situation: "You're the great American institution that never gets mentioned on the Fourth of July: a grass widow. With two small children to raise on your own—the dirty bastard!" (Veda's sister Ray is seven: she is good-natured and eager to please, whereas Veda is supercilious—yet it is on the older daughter's chest that Mildred rests her head before bedtime.)

Mildred has a fling with Bert's burly former business partner, Wally Burgan (James LeGros). Quite unlike any other leading female character in Haynes's films, with the partial exception of Nancy in "Horror," Mildred is vivaciously sexual and comfortable in her skin. At one point she laughs out loud as she and Wally flop on the bed; it makes quite a change from the perfunctory grinding at the start of *Safe*. Later, *Mildred Pierce* includes prolonged sex scenes between Mildred and Monty (Guy Pearce) that are unprecedented in the director's work. (The nearest parallels are much less exuberant lovemaking in "Homo" and *Velvet Goldmine*.)

She interviews to be a housekeeper for a Hollywood director, but his gold-satin-attired middle-aged fiancée, Mrs. Forrester (Hope Davis), is a snob—"It's customary, Mildred, for the servant to sit on the mistress's invitation, not on her own initiative"—and Mildred walks out. Having worn her ankles raw job-hunting, she stops for a ham sandwich at Cristofor's Cafe. After an argument between two waitresses about pilfered tips leads to the pair of them being fired, Mildred impulsively offers her services. The boss, Mr. Chris (Mark Margolis), agrees, though the manager, Ida Corwin (Mare Winningham), is less impressed with the new recruit. When Veda finds out her mother's new occupation in part 2, she is scornful. Mildred spanks her, then backs down by claiming that she is just gaining on-the-job experience before opening her own restaurant—a scheme she proceeds, with Wally's help, to hatch.

The day Mildred leaves Cristofor's, lean, dapper, floppy-haired Monty orders breakfast and flirts, inviting her to his beach house. They have glorious sex, but the rapture is short-lived. Mildred gets home to discover that her younger daughter is in the hospital. There Ray succumbs precipitously to influenza. At home, Mildred crawls into bed with her surviving child and sobs, "Veda, Veda, oh thank God"—consumed by what the novel calls "a guilty, leaping joy that it had been the other child who was taken from her, and not Veda" (124).

Mildred makes a success of her chicken-and-waffles restaurant in part 3. Monty attends the opening night and clicks with Veda. He directs her to a sought-after piano teacher, Charlie Hannen (Richard Easton). With the repeal of Prohibition, Lucy opens a bar at Mildred's, joining a team that includes Ida too. Success allows Mildred to support Monty when his business goes bust. With finances stretched, she does not buy Veda a grand piano for Christmas, and they fight again. Veda mocks Mildred with something Monty has confided: "The very best legs are found in kitchens, not in drawing rooms: never take the mistress if you can get the maid." Mildred drives through a storm to end the affair with her indiscreet paramour.

Time has passed: it is 1937 when part 4 begins, and Mildred is adding a new beachside restaurant in Laguna to her growing chain. Wally persuades her to protect the business: "If you incorporate, your personal property's safe from anyone." Veda is now a stunning, auburn-haired eighteen-year-old. When Hannen dies, she tries out for Carlo Treviso (Ronald Guttman), but he snubs her. She shouts at Mildred later: "You think I'm hot stuff, don't you? You, lying there every day dreaming about rainbows. Well I'm not. I'm just a Glendale Wunderkind, and there's one like me in every Glendale on earth, every one-horse conservatory, every tank-town university, every park band. We can read anything, play anything, arrange anything—but we're no damned good! Punks! Just like you. God, now I know where I get it from. Isn't it funny: you start off a Wunderkind, and you end up just a goddamn punk."

Mrs. Lenhardt, formerly Mrs. Forrester, comes to visit Mildred and accuses Veda of trying to entrap her son into marriage. Veda's subsequent explanation is that she is pregnant; given Mrs. Lenhardt's disapproval, Wally is negotiating a settlement with the wealthy movie family. Later Veda admits that the pregnancy talk was a con. Mildred explodes and orders her out. A few months later, even Lucy is transfixed by the sound of Veda singing "The Bell Song" from *Lakmé* on the Hank Somerville (Pleasant Cigarettes) radio program, while Mildred is almost petrified.

At the start of part 5, Mildred cannot persuade Treviso, who is now Veda's impresario, to let her pay for her daughter's coaching. As she is driven away, disgruntled Mildred spots Monty on a street corner and gets an idea that is spelled out in the novel: "Just how exact her plan was it would be hard to say. She was wholly feminine, and it seems to be part of the feminine mind that it can tack indefinitely upwind, each tack bearing off at a vague angle, and yet all bearing inexorably on the buoy. Perhaps she herself didn't quite know how many tacks she would have to make to reach the buoy, which was Veda, not Monty" (239). The reunited lovers refurbish Monty's Pasadena mansion according to his axioms: "Whatever pertains to comfort, shoot the works. But with whatever pertains to show, be a little modest. People like you better if you aren't so *damned* rich." On their wedding night Veda returns to this upscale residence to sing the wedding march. When all the guests have gone, Mildred goes into her daughter's room and kisses her worshipfully while she sleeps.

"Mildred now entered the days of her apotheosis," according to the novel. "War was crashing in Europe, but she knew little of it, and cared less. She was drunk with the glory of the Valhalla she had entered: the house among the oaks, where dwelt the girl with the coppery hair, the lovely voice, and the retinue of admirers, teachers, coaches, agents, and thieves who made life so exciting" (254). As a duplicitous encore to a concert at the Philharmonic Auditorium, Veda performs her mother's favorite song, "I'm Always Chasing Rainbows," and Mildred is ravished once more. She is blind to the renewed complicity between Veda and Monty. When Mildred arrives at the Philharmonic, Monty is there ahead of her in Veda's dressing room. And a moment before the encore, her husband whispers with foreknowledge: "This one's just for you."

Mildred's lavish new lifestyle, financed by money surreptitiously drained from the business, leads to her being summoned to a creditors' meeting by Wally. It is followed by a showdown with Veda during which Mildred, outraged when she discovers the affair with Monty, tries to strangle her. *Mildred Pierce* ends with Mildred and Bert remarrying. On her way to join Monty in New York, Veda stops by the old house, to which the newlyweds have returned. In what may be her final conversation with Mildred, she, like Karen, Richie, and Arthur, takes her leave, but this time the story stays with the parents.

After Veda's departure, Mildred almost doubles over with grief, stumbling down the road. "To hell with her," says Bert at the end, in the secluded safe space of the first restaurant. "We've got each other, haven't we? Let's get stinko," he says with a smile, and Mildred gives her maudlin assent: "Yes. Let's get stinko." This call-and-response recalls Veda's spiteful declaration to Mildred in part 4: "I can get away from . . . every rotten, stinking thing that even reminds me of this place or you," but it also brings back lines from *Velvet Goldmine*'s opening voiceover— "Jack would discover that somewhere there were others quite like him, singled out for a great gift, and one day the whole stinking world would be theirs"—as well as Graves's rooftop peroration in "Horror" about "the kind of misery the whole stinking world is made of." Oppression everywhere, defiance, and servile resignation: the permutations of the stench metaphor map the main themes of Haynes's work.

Brilliant Careers

A dreamy scene in *Velvet Goldmine* marks the beginning of Brian's climb to superstardom. It is New Year's Eve 1969 outside the Sombrero Club. With Mahler playing on the sound track, the future idol's approach to the club door is filmed in a point-of-view shot. After someone wearing a satin cape is waved in by the doorman, Cooper (Joseph Beattie), it is Brian's turn, but the gatekeeper shows no largesse. "That's ten bob to you, mate," and Brian has to dig for coins. The enchantment is broken by the mention of money, but at the same time the scene is spellbound because the Sombrero is the focus of Brian's ambition. He is going to work. When Mildred decides on the spur of the moment to offer her services at Cristofor's, Haynes again switches to a point-of-view shot, this time in slow motion. Mildred's suddenly entranced gaze takes in the bar counter with its display of cakes (which soon she will supply) before moving around the corner into the kitchen. Carter Burwell's solemn and ceremonious music here even has a touch of Mahler. Just a couple of minutes before, Mildred was sweaty on an L.A. bus, worn out and fed up; now she is turned on. The intensity of her induction discloses the desire that pours into her work. Cristofor's has no underground glam mystique, but it is Mildred's Sombrero (during the part 3 commentary, Haynes explains that he wanted to depict the opening night of Mildred's like a backstage musical).

Cristofor's is an austerity workplace. It costs to work there, just as it costs Brian to get into the nightclub. Ida explains: "Your uniform comes off the first check: $3.95, and you keep the garment. The pay is twenty-five cents an hour, and you keep your own tips." (At the end of part 1, Lucy does the math: "Those tips'll bring in a couple of dollars a day, and before you know it you'll be making fifteen, twenty dollars a week at least.") Yet Mildred thrives during the Depression (as Veda eventually does too). She proves herself industrious, capable; she has a head for business. The first restaurant is all about efficiency: "It seems as though it ought to pay. That's the main thing, Wally, about this idea of mine. What costs in a restaurant is waste, and the extras like the printing for the menus and the people you have to have for the features you put in, but this way there wouldn't be any waste." Like the novel, the miniseries pays attention to minutiae such as the $46.37 Mildred pays for twenty-four chickens in part 3.

Mildred starts out a good employee, seizes an opportunity, and becomes an entrepreneur—a self-made woman—with additional prowess in delegating and managing. It is no surprise that when she talks about politics, her opinions reflect can-do diligence. She expresses support for Franklin D. Roosevelt in part 4: "I'm voting for him because somebody's gotta put an end to all this Hoover extravagance and balance this budget. And all those people demanding help. You can't tell me people couldn't get along even if there is a depression if only they had a little gump." But she is not emotionally detached: when the business grows through the 1930s, she teams up with her best friends. (Mildred's husbands are less reliable. Bert seems to live off Mrs. Biederhof, until she returns to her long-forgotten husband after he strikes oil in Texas, at which point Bert moves in with his parents. And Monty's approach to work is described by Haynes during the part 3 commentary as exemplifying the "blueblood tradition of noblesse oblige and of kind of fantasizing your way through life and projecting projects, but not having to work to pay the bills.")

The pride Mildred takes in her work leads her to a kind of reverse snobbery. It is true that she pushes Veda up the social ladder—in part 4 she is delighted by Veda's airy suggestion that she might be going into pictures—but when she rubs up against Hollywood aristocracy in the chic personage of Mrs. Lenhardt, she looks down her own nose at the director's pretentious wife, who makes such a fuss about etiquette. "The mistress terminates the interview, Mildred," says the prospective employer during their first meeting in part 1. "Mrs. Pierce, if you don't mind, and I'm terminating it," Mildred replies firmly. A similar middle-class impatience with high-society affectation is evident when, in part 3, Mildred picks Veda up from Monty's polo club. Spectators in hats drink champagne at park tables; smartly dressed servants stand around. Mildred instinctively adjusts her jacket and fixes her expression; she does not fit in here. In the video interview for the HBO Web site, Haynes parsed the scene: "She gains access to this man and his world and his culture, which means everything to this daughter whose love she covets and desires, and yet there's a boundary drawn between those worlds." Veda's access is subsidized by Mildred—Haynes mentioned her "secret labor that's supporting and propping up this value that her daughter aspires to"—but nothing suggests that Mildred herself has any desire for the grand life of leisure. It just annoys her.

Mildred's disdain and indignation return at the creditors' meeting in part 5: "Wally, neither you nor anybody else has the right to take what belongs to me or what belongs to my child to pay the bills of this business. Maybe you've forgotten, Mr. Wally Burgan, that it was you who told me to incorporate for precisely this reason—to keep my personal property safe from any creditor." Her sometime lover retorts: "You're right no one here can take a dime of your money or Veda's—all they can do is go to court, have you declared bankrupt, and take over. Court'll appoint receivers, and you'll be out." This duly happens, with Ida apologetically taking charge, but Mildred's pride is not dented. Her work ethic and independence are the traits that balance her wilder side. Haynes's Mildred is not a character like Joan Crawford's Lane, in Curtiz's *Flamingo Road* (1949), who quits waitressing to marry into money. Mildred has more in common with another Crawford heroine, Vienna in *Johnny Guitar* (1954), who boldly asserts her autonomy in Nicholas Ray's Western. "This was free country when I came. I'm not giving up a single foot of it," she says to unscrupulous locals. "You don't own the earth, not this part of it."

Some of *Mildred Pierce*'s resonance for the time of its release derives from the difference between Mildred and Veda when it comes to work, since the contrast reflects a contemporary trend. Veda is not, except for a lack of anything better to do, and only for as long as it suits her, an idler. She is smart, dedicated, and a superb planner. This makes her a talented con artist. During her spell hanging out with Hollywood kids, she is lining up the Lenhardt family for the fake-pregnancy scam. But after she discovers her singing ability, her true and miraculous artistry, she switches from crook to skillful freelancer with a real flair for the negotiating skill that her mother disdains. In part 5, the ascendant coloratura is angry when Mo Levinson (Daniel London), her manager, turns down a two-year, $2,500-a-week contract from the president of Consolidated Foods to promote Sunbake vitamin bread. Says Mo: "She's sold. She sings for Pleasant, the mentholated cigarettes"—for a mere five hundred dollars a week. "Sorry, kid, a contract's a contract. You signed on the dotted line, nothing to do about that." When she continues to complain, he retaliates by threatening to give prestigious work to another client, at which point Veda turns on a dime—pragmatism overriding pride—and apologizes tactically. Faced with Mo's toughness, Veda backs down graciously, regroups, and at the end of part 5 finds a route to the better deal with amazing, intuitive savoir-faire: when she stops by the remarriage party, her mother realizes that Veda exaggerated her injury after the strangling attempt in order to get out of the deal that prevented her from signing with Consolidated Foods. The novel has more detail about the maneuver: Pleasant sues "to have the contract annulled, on the ground that Veda was no longer able to fulfil it" (278), and Mildred fills in the gaps, "You didn't lose any voice, you just thought faster than anybody else" (280).

Mildred is haughty about contracts; Veda respects or gets the better of them. The emphasis on business and contracts neutralizes the noir double-cross. In Curtiz's film, in a scene with no basis in the novel, treachery is played up. Monte detects that Mildred is using him to lure Veda, and she admits it: "My businesslike air isn't fooling you much, is it?" ("Your reason for doing anything is usually Veda," he remarks.) They negotiate over a stake in Mildred's empire with only minimum tact. "How much of a share would your pride require, Monte?" "One third," he replies, and Mildred agrees derisively: "Alright—sold, one Beragon." Then, at the creditors' meeting, Wally (Jack Carson) takes her aside to explain: "You'd still be alright if Monte hadn't forced the situation. . . . I thought you knew this was his idea. He wants to sell his share of the business, and I have to go along or I'm out too." Mildred is slightly dazed. As the meeting breaks up, one of the participants, Jones (Chester Clute), says: "I'm sorry this has happened, but if I do say it, as perhaps I shouldn't, I think Mr. Beragon acted badly, very badly indeed." (Fassbinder's noir-influenced 1979 *The Marriage of Maria Braun*, whose resourceful title character is similar to Mildred in achieving career success, plays a variation on this betrayal by contract: Maria discovers that her jailed husband did a deal with her rich lover—agreeing not to get in the way of the affair in return for a share in the lover's business.)

In Haynes's *Mildred Pierce*, the double-cross is shrunk back to an unconvincing moment after the creditors' meeting when Mildred and Bert suddenly sense a hidden hand. Bert says: "Mildred, you can't trust Wally Burgin, not even till the sun comes up. He was my pal, and he crossed me. He was your pal, and he crossed you. But he was Veda's pal too, Mildred, and maybe he's getting ready to cross her too, and somehow get his hands on her dough. . . . How can we believe anything that guy says? Maybe that meeting today was just a phony. Maybe he's getting ready to compel you to take her money, as her guardian, so he can attack it. She's still a minor, you know. Mildred, you're seeing her tonight, and you're getting her out of that house before any process server can find her, you understand me?" Suddenly *Mildred Pierce* seems to have entered the thriller's suspicious and swindling domain, but, in a further twist, the brief spell of paranoia is nothing more than the plot device needed to give Mildred a reason to find Veda late at night.

If You Don't Know Me by Now

The Veda-on-the-radio scene has a parallel in Pedro Almodóvar's *High Heels* (1991), which reworks *Imitation of Life* and Curtiz's *Mildred Pierce*. In the Spanish film, the scene is turned around: the broadcast voice is that of a diva mother, Becky (Marisa Paredes), in concert, while the listener is her daughter Rebeca (Victoria Abril), jailed for murdering her husband. "I don't care what she has done," declares Becky. "I am her mother, and my heart is shattered. If you don't mind, I would like to dedicate the first song to her." "Think of Me" is a song of fidelity, but for some reason—maybe she is too moved by the evidence of her mother's concern, or perhaps she detects that Rebeca is enjoying the scandal's limelight—Becky is unnerved and asks for the radio to be turned off. "I can't stand listening to her," she says. Later, incensed, she confesses her resentment. First she mentions a scene in Bergman's *Autumn Sonata* (1978), in which a concert pianist points out the deficiencies of her own daughter's playing, and then Becky's rancor toward Rebeca emerges: "You promised me that we would enjoy life together, that we'd never be apart, but you didn't keep your promise."

Autumn Sonata presents the relation between mother and daughter as an endless struggle. Bergman's drama builds to an uninhibited late-night argument between Charlotte (Ingrid Bergman) and her disgruntled grownup daughter, Eva (Liv Ullmann), who says: "A mother and her daughter. What a terrible combination of emotions and confusion and destruction. Everything's possible and will be done in the name of love and caring. The daughter shall inherit the mother's injuries. The daughter shall suffer for the mother's failures. The unhappiness of the mother shall be the daughter's unhappiness. It's as if the umbilical cord had never been cut. Is the daughter's unhappiness the mother's triumph? Is my grief your secret pleasure?" Or, given so long-winded and liturgical a pronouncement, is it Eva's own private enjoyment? After Charlotte leaves, her daughter resolves, "I'll never see her again," but she wavers, and *Autumn Sonata* concludes with Eva writing a conciliatory letter: "There is a kind of grace. I mean the opportunity we have to take care of each other, to help each other, to show affection. Never again will I let you disappear from my life." Thus, unless everything is supposed to have changed, so it goes around again in an addictive cycle.

Both *Imitation of Life* and *High Heels* end with mothers dying. In Sirk's film, Sarah Jane realizes the depth of her attachment to Annie only at the funeral: "I'm sorry, mama. Mama, I did love you!" In Almodóvar's, there is just enough time for a tearful reconciliation. "We are living together again," Becky says on her death bed. Are they thus films about mutual passion or love's end? Can love even be taken for granted? When Linda Williams in "Melancholy Melodrama" described *High Heels* as "a melancholic revision of *Mildred Pierce* that acts out the queer incestuous romance that the heteronormative Hollywood classic violently represses at the end" (175), it demonstrated the standard psychoanalytic assumption—also there in Freud's account of masochistic initiation in "'A Child Is Being Beaten'"—that parent and child share an emotional dependency. Non-Oedipal though it is, the queerness of "queer incestuous romance" is a queerness of loyalty that remains within the mansion of family passion.

Less conducive to family-centered analysis, Haynes's films bring into the picture both careful coercion (*Dottie Gets Spanked*) and rebellious apathy: in "Hero," Richie not only kills his father, he also deserts his mother. The three-person family is torn apart. Richie's leave-taking is another kind of queerness—one that disdains, annuls, destroys, and escapes intimate family bondage. (Haynes's films are full of enigmatic or sorrowful solitudes that cannot be emotionally tied. As a director, Haynes has something in common with the author in Almodóvar's 1995 *The Flower of My Secret,* who says: "I can't write rose-tinted novels. They come out black.")

What kind of family romance exists between Mildred and Veda? Time and again, a scene presents high-intensity emotions as home theater. Family relations are improvisations, unless they are just plain artifice. In part 2, mother and daughter have their first severe argument. Veda turns nasty: "Aren't the pies bad enough? Did you have to degrade

Family romance (*Mildred Pierce*).

us all by becoming a waitress?" Mildred spanks her with vigor. Veda shrieks, but as soon as it is over, she is perfectly composed. Mildred weeps and then self-piteously says: "You don't ever give me credit for any finer feelings, do you?" But Veda is having none of it: "Oh Mother, cut the penny-dreadful dramatics." This line is not in Cain's book. In fact, the novel has a role-reversal, referring to "Veda's bland, phony toniness" as opposed to Mildred's authenticity, which Cain takes for granted: "Mildred yearned for warm affection from this child, such as Bert apparently commanded. But all she ever got was a stagy, affected counterfeit" (79). Yet Haynes's Veda has a point. (She makes the same charge at the end of part 4: "Mother, you needn't be *so* overdramatic.") For her mother pulls herself together with aplomb, and the scenario changes quickly. Sighing, Mildred says: "The truth is, I felt exactly the same as you, but I never would have taken the job to begin with if it hadn't been that I—I've decided to open a place of my own, and had to learn the business from the ground up . . . there's money in a restaurant." Mildred invents the restaurant scheme off the cuff, and as she does so, her anger theatrically turns into a maudlin protest at being misjudged. Veda gladly plays along this time: "Oh, Mother. Mother, forgive me for being so wretched before. I'm sorry I acted so horribly. I think it's just wonderful, just wonderful what you're planning, truly I do." Then they can embrace tenderly, the rancorous parts over. The spanking that leaves Veda so untroubled is thus rather like the one that occurs in the TV studio in *Dottie Gets Spanked*: both Dottie and her stand-in are not brutalized by, or even emotionally involved in, the scene of punishment—because it is a sitcom fiction.

In the even fiercer Christmas argument in episode 3, the miniseries retains a small detail from the novel: "Veda picked up a package of the cigarettes Mildred kept on hand for Monty, lit one, and threw the match on the floor" (169). Onscreen, though, it is bizarre when Veda, dressed in shiny pajamas, with a red ribbon in her hair, self-consciously and amateur-dramatically smokes. Referring to scenes in the mansion during the part 5 commentary, Haynes says: "These scenes always feel to me like they're playing house, which of course they are . . . they're pretending to be these rich people in this new life. . . . Even Monty, it's all part of a kind of dress-up game . . . but it gives it a slight uncertainty, like there's a faultline . . . that they're standing on that's going to give—it doesn't feel genuine or innate." It is not just these scenes, though. Much of the interaction between Mildred and Veda has a just-pretending quality. Both of them role-play, sometimes different parts in the same scene: family emotions seem more like acting than acting out. It is a slightly mesmerizing quality, funny and scary at the same time, which mixes up penny-dreadfulness with a more serious sense of family relations as charades rather than ardent intimacies rooted in the psychoanalytic romance.

There is an escalating progression of scenes in which either Mildred or Veda is, mid-argument, baffled by something the other one says—like actors who remember their lines but not their motivation. They do not behave like they really know each other; both psychological affinity and shared family history seem to be missing. Incomprehension occurs in part 3 when Veda discloses Monty's indiscreet talk about sex and canoodling with a caterer: "Try as he will with his slumming, his shoes are still custom-made." Mildred snaps back: "They ought to be. They cost me enough." Veda is utterly surprised, and her mother enjoys the moment: "You didn't know that, did you?" Later, during the argument in part 4 that ends with Veda leaving home, Mildred realizes that Veda's pregnancy is just a blackmailer's device: "Young lady," she says "you have kept me entirely in the dark on this matter, and I refuse to take any more." Tempers flare and abate, then there is a digression. Out of the blue, Veda accuses her mother of having married Bert for money. Mildred is utterly perplexed: "What money?!" (The scene with Mildred and Bert after the creditors' meeting confirms that Veda made a mistake.) The two of them are closed books to each other. Yet when they find out about their missing knowledge, it is less the discovery of an intricate secret (like the one in *Chinatown*) and more like coming upon a blank: who-lessness rather than whodunit.

The relationship between mother and daughter in Haynes's *Mildred Pierce* is disorienting and incongruous rather than entwined and close—a crossword puzzle with misprinted clues rather than a family passion; a block of ice, not a tangled web. The scenes between Mildred and Veda confound the psychoanalytic presumption of intimacy. In so doing, they reflect back to that widely held paradigm its own perversity in insisting on the emotional pull of either pathos or antipathy, which rules out the apathy that Veda shares with Richie in "Hero." Mother and daughter often lie to each other in the miniseries, but the open lie—the opposite of an open secret—which is the ghost in the room when they tussle, is that their intimacy is null and void, fraudulent.

Two scenes of effacement personify this hard-to-read emptiness. In part 5, Mildred watches her ascendant daughter perform at the Philharmonic—a performance that will conclude with the love hoax of Veda's cynical encore rendition of "I'm Always Chasing Rainbows." Before that, Mildred peers through opera glasses to get a better look at the coloratura, who is dressed somewhat absurdly in serpent green, with a coiffure of ringlets—a veritable parody of Treviso's earlier characterization of her as a snake. While she is singing Mozart's "Hell's Vengeance Boils in My Heart" from *The Magic Flute,* Mildred raises her opera glasses to get a closer look, flinches at Veda's merciless expression, and abruptly puts the binoculars down again. Haynes comments that Mildred "sees a little too much of Veda's attitude, and opts out for the euphoria of distance that she can fill in." But is it a personality trait on view or a simulation? Rather than naked proof of intrinsic hostility, the look on Veda's face is a dramatic accouterment—and one veering toward the comic, like the preposterous parasol that she carries at the start of the recital. The aria is angry, so Veda's expression is in character. This is one thespian visage among many. It is her daughter's capacity to wear a mask—not only on stage but at home, and perhaps with nothing underneath—that is so hard for Mildred to behold because it shines a light on all the domestic playacting too, at which Mildred is herself so proficient, though she can never admit it. What appears in the sights of the opera glasses is a device from intimacy's repertoire of techniques that does not even require proximity. As Veda herself puts it during her preparation for the concert: "There are two thousand seats in that place, and they've all got to feel like I'm one of them."

The Philharmonic scene recalls the ambiguous incorporation of the *Flesh and Fantasy* clip in *Superstar.* Mildred looks for a credible person— her daughter, preferably a loving daughter who adores her—and recoils from the sight of something more mechanical, less meaningful. Haynes comments as Veda finishes the encore: "She really, truly looks like the porcelain princess from hell." It is a jokey remark, but as in *Superstar,* the loss of distinctive signs that make a psychologically readable person is a horror show too.

The ambiguous image of Veda eavesdropping that ends part 1 is an ink-blot test of the psychoanalytic family-romance presumption. The shot shows clandestine surveillance, reviving noir's knowledge games, the criss-cross of suspicion, betrayal, and intrigue. It shows a listening-in, and, from the point of view of the domestic interior, it confirms the magnetic family's pull on attention. But the image shows something less too. The slightly out-of-focus bars distance the faceless figure outside the household, looking away. It is an image of impersonality and departure, and it is dominated by oval shapes: the curved iron, the crown of Veda's head, the maritime collar of her dress with its design of hoops, even the stray curls of her red hair. These shapes make a pattern of zeros—of noughts rather than double-crosses. At the end of part 3, the shot is reenacted after the argument about the Lenhardts, nonpregnancy, and money. This time, when the camera dollies toward the ironwork there is no one there. Veda has gone, but was she ever at home?

Funeral Home

The miniseries depicts household space as constricted and removed. Red-dotted half-drapes keep the light dim in the parlor of the fraught Pierce home; net curtains are drawn at the front; and there are the ornamental bars in front of the side door that Veda eavesdrops outside of. The windows keep out as much as they let in. At the beginning of part 1, the camera pans along a door whose glass panels are slightly pebbled; they blur, like a heat haze, the image of Bert mowing the lawn. Bouncy jazz plays on the sound track, but it only partly offsets the disorienting impression of the outside world being hallucinatory, a mirage when viewed from so immersive a household. The blurring happens again on Lucy's first appearance. As she walks toward the back door, the pressed glass makes her slightly fluid, out of focus: she does not seem solid until she enters. The relationship between inside and outside is distorted. When Mildred and Monty first go to the mansion in part 5, the downstairs room with its grand chandelier is dominated by a picture window. Its ornate frame makes the glaringly bright shrubbery beyond seem like a Technicolor rear projection.

Monty tells Mildred in part 5, not unkindly, that her Glendale living room was "the worst room I was ever in" because "not one thing in it, until that piano came, ever meant a thing to you . . . or anybody else." Haynes's preoccupation with the incarceration of everyday life is overlaid in *Mildred Pierce* with grief at life not lived as a consequence. The extended family gathers at the beginning of part 3 for Ray's funeral. (It is strange to see Mildred greet her own mother, played by Lillian Lifflander.) Two shots during this scene inscribe mourning into the very texture of the image. First, Bert is filmed from outside the window, staring through slightly smeared glass in frozen sorrow. Then, when Ray's grandparents arrive in mourning clothes, their approach to the house is once more filmed through a barred window. This one has black net curtains, and the profound poignancy of the guarded, grief-struck image encompasses both a child's untimely death and a mournful darkening of everything the domestic bastion excludes.

Mildred meets Monty on her last day working at Cristofor's, which makes it easier for her to act on impulse and join him for a trip to Santa Barbara. Wearing sunglasses in the convertible as they speed along, she is youthfully exhilarated: "I can't quite believe I'm doing this." At his beach house, Monty banters amiably until he suddenly realizes that his guest has just run out over the sand, and so he chases after her, much as Monte does in the 1945 film. In Curtiz's version, the camera is an outdoor spectator to this foreplay, and, after a cut, it gets up close to the amorous couple from a vantage point right at the edge of the sea, joyous and jaunty incidental music accompanying. By contrast, the only playful thing about Haynes's version is the jokey title of Burwell's music, "Mounting Monty." The tune itself lives up to neither this jokiness nor the exuberance of the beach frolics. It is elegiac—music to suit not what the lovers are doing but how what they are doing is framed. The camera does not leave the building this time; instead there is a slow zoom toward the window. Seconds later, Mildred and Monty are far away, no longer even identifiable, this carefree interlude standing for everything that the mostly housebound and curtained-off story cannot represent except as the miasma of what gets lost in the distance.

Out of It

Mildred senses that her husband is hiding something, and so she pushes past him. Inside the tack room, she sees her beautiful daughter in Monty's bed. The musical score is dreary, droning, discordant—like a speckled vortex of white noise instrumented into the rudiments of melody. Mildred's voice is little more than a whisper: "Oh, oh, oh God." They are words of shock and trauma, but Veda refuses their emotional insinuation. The oil spill of pathos simply cannot spread. "Mother," says the teenager with steel. The way the word is enunciated entails no dutiful recognition, no guilty acknowledgment. "Mother" does not identify Mildred as a person but as a tiresomely predictable type. Mannered dialogue previously embellished the open lie of their intimacy, but now Veda shuts conversation down (her remaining lines refer to her mother in the third person), and Mildred cannot say a word against it. She has only four more syllables in the whole astonishing scene, and they are uttered to Monty. The first three are ineffectively defensive: "How could you?" He is suddenly garrulous—prattling, rationalizing, psychologizing, justifying, thinking out loud, like someone talking back at a TV set: "You thought you hold the strings on everybody, didn't you? You thought you could come around and dress me up and use me as bait to lure your famous daughter back to the teat." Mildred is left to emit a mere mumbled "no."

Monty's references to dress-up and puppetry are not in the novel. They preview the much more severe negation that comes next: Veda's wordless enactment of apathy, her Theater of No. Her naked parade when she gets out of bed is a denial of family affection's protocols of decency, but the uncanniness of her movement is not just catwalk-ceremonious; it is robotic. Princess Veda has become a porcelain Terminator. She looks directly back at her mother, strides slowly to the dressing table, sits down . . . and starts to comb her hair. So first she meets Mildred's gaze, then she feigns her toilette as if her mother were not watching. Pointedly, Veda does more than ignore; she lures Mildred's look in order to deny it. Her meant-to-be-seen silent routine insists that her mother bear witness to being excluded from the scene, from Veda's life. Mildred has to follow a demonstration that her dollhouse family romance is wishful thinking.

It is a figment, phantom intimacy, and it always was. Veda demands that Mildred recognize her own fiction-making for what it is, and in so doing exposes the worthlessness of her mother's precious counterfeit archive. Veda's ruthless slow solo mime of repudiation impacts retroactively, going back in time like the twisted score at the beginning of the scene. For, Haynes comments: "Carter literally took the pastoral music that plays when Monty and Mildred first have sex in episode 2 at the

beach house—that kind of lyrical, floaty piece that's very, very tranquil
. . . and he inverted it and played it backwards." It is a kind of filial re-
venge, but also a pedagogy—or a mutant psychoanalysis, with neither
talk nor cure.

After Ray died, and then after her wedding, Mildred wanted nothing
more than to find her daughter in bed in the dark. If she remembers
now these other solemn nighttime visits to Veda, the trouble is that
Veda has no corresponding memories of them because she was sleeping.
Mother and daughter are not secret sharers: there is only a dark blur at
the heart of their relation. For much too long Mildred relied on one-
way-mirror intimacy, and when Veda now peers back through the glass,
it is an unspeakable humiliation of her mother because Mildred has to
realize that there is—and can have been—no reconciliation of, or even
significant overlap between, the ambits of their incongruous dumb-show
memories and survival stories. Veda demands, impossibly, that Mildred
stop pretending they are in the same room of their house of pain—that
she understand that, in Veda's outlook, she was never more than a dark
and fleeting shape on the fringe, as Veda herself was when Mildred
watched her silhouette from the street. It is no wonder that Mildred
dives forward to throttle her daughter, until Monty intervenes and Veda
can run downstairs. The coloratura soprano wheezes then vomits when
she gets to the grand piano downstairs, and squawks rather than sings
as she kneels on the piano stool before falling, weeping, to the ground.

"I wonder if the world's to blame / I wonder if it could be me" are
lyrics from "I'm Always Chasing Rainbows," and one self-help solution
to the conundrum is given by Peter in *Safe*: "When you look out on the
world from a place of love and a place of forgiveness, what you are seeing
outside is a reflection of what you feel within." This idea was inculcated
in Carol in the form of baby-talk self-affirmations, flower words, and
Mildred would speak them now if she could. But with the manipulative sociability of language having become, in the penultimate scene of
Mildred Pierce, murmurs, grunts, screeches, wails, and retching, there
are no garlands to decorate the safe-house walls as they close in.

Cain wrote in the novel, "They made in truth a ghastly procession, and
the grey light that filtered in seemed the only conceivable illumination for
the hatred that twisted their faces" (276), but Haynes ends the scene with
facelessness. The score's scratchy chamber music sounds like a medieval

Back in line (*Mildred Pierce*).

dirge played on period instruments that have not been properly tuned. It is the world's turn at vengeance now. This apocalypse ends with a fade on an image of the family snapped back into line. It is a left-to-right flip of the scene in *Dottie Gets Spanked* in which, framed from a similar elevation, Stevie's parents challenge his TV-viewing. Knocked-out, prostrate, Veda is far in the background, her hair spilling on the floor, as if she has been sacrificed next to the piano. Mildred is in the middle, hunched, trembling, her arms folded. Behind her, in the extreme foreground, is shellshocked Monty. They are all turned away, but fixed together in a chain gang. It is an image of unending institutional clampdown. As the three of them are ingrained in the gloom, they are deathlike dolls locked in intimacy. It is, after everything, a true family romance. The fade on the image is agonizingly slow, and a nightmare inversion of the whiteout finale of "Hero," because this time there is no flight and because it comes out black.

Epilogue

In Haynes's films, the misery the world is made of is not uniform. The cinematic realm can appear as dollhouse, trash city, acrimonious suburbia, dystopian metropolis, or most often of all, haunted domicile. To be in such a world is to be trapped, perhaps without recognizing this plight. Or to exist there is to get used to the situation, settle down, make a home obediently. (But only in *I'm Not There* is domesticity jarringly represented as good.) If need be, a masochistic swindle can be accomplished, secret pleasure stolen from the condition of subservience. The chance of something more than such a con trick—the chance of escape—is complicated in Haynes's films by treacherous refuges that are no better than their alternative: Karen's condo, Baton, Wrenwood, the wonderland of glam, Billy's Missouri. *Far from Heaven* presents nothing else except a false sanctuary.

The shadow of suicide falls on Haynes's work, but Graves's hopeless deathbound plunge into the mob in "Horror" is only part of the clouded picture. The paradoxically self-multiplying rock 'n' roll suicides in *Velvet Goldmine* and *I'm Not There* count too, as do the too-early queer funeral that concludes *Dottie Gets Spanked* and Karen's death-driven anorexic obsession. More enigmatic and radical are the semi-suicides of Richie in "Hero" and Carol in *Safe,* which are disappearances, vanishing acts (never completed in Carol's case), defiant fadeouts, not socially enforced sacrificial penalties. They belong to the order of transgressive experience that is invoked by Artaud in "On Suicide": "I feel death upon me like a torrent, like an instantaneous bound of lightning whose capacity surpasses my imagination. I feel a death loaded with pleasures, with swirling labyrinths. Where is the idea of my being therein?" (57). They also both involve repudiation of family life—total for Richie, tentative for Carol before she is recaptured.

Haynes wrote in the introduction to *Three Screenplays*: "I agree with Fassbinder who said, 'Revolution doesn't belong on the cinema screen, but outside, in the world.' To provide an audience with a solution—to give them the revolution—is to deprive them of the necessity of creating their own. 'Never mind if a film ends pessimistically,' he said, 'if it explores certain mechanisms clearly enough to show people how exactly they work, then the ultimate effect is not pessimistic.' I've always felt that viewers of film have extraordinary powers: they can make life out of reflections on the wall. Perhaps it's in the spaces we allow them to reflect (upon) themselves that films encourage these powers of transformation to continue—even after the movie is over" (xii). Or perhaps, in the wake-up-call context of the way his films envisage myriad forms of social and environmental imprisonment, it is in fragmentary gestures toward the power of disappearance, not transformation, and of the death which Artaud speaks of, not life, that Todd Haynes gives the viewer more than he was ready to admit.

Is it possible that, like spectral Carol in the garden, Mildred is following a line of flight when she walks away from the radio in *Mildred Pierce*? That seems at first unlikely. The scene appears to be the apogee of family mania, a version of the drowned-by-voices scene in *Superstar*, long-distance emotional ties dominating a scene. In Cain's novel, the emotion does not go off the scale. The scene is one of calculated determination to be reunited: "Pushing through the bushes, she reached the bluff overlooking the sea, and stood there, lacing her fingers together, screwing her lips into a thin, relentless line. This, she needed nobody to tell her, was no descent from Beethoven to Hank Somerville, no cheap venture into torch. It was the coming true of all she had dreamed for Veda, all she had believed in, worked for, dedicated her life to. The only difference was that the dream that had come true was a thousand times rosier than the dream she had dreamed. And come what may, by whatever means she would have to take, she knew she would have to get Veda back" (231–32). Mildred is still less affected at this point in Curtiz's film: she is impassively disapproving as she watches Veda hula and croon in Wally's seedy nightclub.

The melodramatic emotion in Haynes's scene has, though, a precedent in *Imitation of Life*. Sirk's film includes a scene in which Annie

On the verge (*Mildred Pierce*).

discovers Sarah Jane performing a risqué song-and-dance number in dingy Harry's Club in New York. (There is no equivalent in John M. Stahl's 1934 film of the same story: the daughter is not a singer but a restaurant hostess.) Annie is fierce but self-possessed during her nightclub confrontation, admonishing her daughter for the pretense of working as a librarian. "Never seen her before in my life," says Sarah Jane unconvincingly to the boss. Annie trumps her: "If you don't tell her to go home with me, her mother, I'll have the law on you!" But outside the emotions escalate when Sarah Jane strides away. Annie calls after her, but then suddenly weakens and has to sit down on some steps while she weeps. In Fassbinder's notes on Sirk, he made comments on *Imitation of Life* that apply perfectly to this scene, and also to Haynes's *Mildred Pierce*: "The mother who wants to possess her child because she loves her is brutal. And Sarah Jane is defending herself against her mother's terrorism, the world's terrorism. That's cruel; you can understand both of them, and both of them are right, and no one will ever be able to help either of them. Unless, of course, we change the world. We cried over the movie. Because it's so hard to change the world" (89).

Suicide haunts the terror and tears at the end of part 4 of the miniseries because of an indirect link back to Curtiz's film. Right at the beginning of the 1945 version, after the opening scene-of-the-crime flashback, Mildred is lost in melancholy thought as she walks along the lamplit pier outside Wally's joint. Like Winslet's Mildred, she places her hands on the rail to steady herself. The sound of the sea can be heard beneath the orchestral score. As Mildred looks down, a policeman approaches. She leans forward, and the cop immediately hits the metal rail with his nightstick. He shines his torch in her face then says, "What's on your mind, lady? You know what I think? I think maybe you had an idea you'd take a swim." Mildred replies, "Leave me alone." The cop is unmoved and reminds her of her social responsibility. "You take a swim, I'd have to take a swim. Is that fair? Just 'cause you feel like bumping yourself off, I gotta get pneumonia? Never thought about that, did ya? Okay, think about it. Go on, beat it. Go on home before we both take a swim." And off Mildred goes, leaving the cop to write something in his notebook.

There is a rerecording technique in film sound called worldizing. It was used by Haynes in *Mildred Pierce* for the scenes in which Veda is seen lip-synching to opera (usually sung by Sumi Jo), as he explains during the part 5 commentary on the wedding scene when Veda surprises Mildred by singing for the newlyweds: "We had a great sound team that actually took these recordings, and anything that was going to be played in a live room [was] worldized, which is where you play back the recording in the room and rerecord it in the ambience of the room, with the natural echo and distance, so the sound of Veda's voice coming from inside that's manipulated and gets louder and then finally is attached to [Veda's] lips is incredibly effective." The soundscape of the scene is engineered to evoke the perception of the characters onscreen: when Veda starts singing while Mildred and Monty are on the terrace, she is almost out of Mildred's earshot, and accordingly the sound is faint. Then, as the couple approaches the source, the singing gets louder; the miniseries' audience hears what Mildred hears.

But this does not happen at the end of part 4. If Veda's radio broadcast were worldized, it would fade as Mildred heads for the lamplit jetty. Instead, the volume of "The Bell Song" holds steady as Veda sings about ostracism. (Mildred stands during the part of the libretto by Edmond Gondinet and Philippe Gille that translates as: "She runs over the moss / And she doesn't remember / That everywhere is shunned / The child of the pariahs.") Yet the music has not been entirely detached from the story, because the sound of waves intrudes as Mildred walks toward the sea. The playback of "The Bell Song" accommodates the natural noise but is not itself adjusted to accord with what Mildred would hear (the radio subsiding as the waves grow louder). The two sound sources intermingle without the onscreen listener's presence being also factored into the acoustic environment. Mildred has fallen out of the world. She's not there.

It is a moment set apart, no longer governed by the storytelling. The night and the sea are beautiful and empty. The miserable cage world is behind Mildred Pierce as she stands on the Laguna shore with no one to remind her of obligation. The family line is completely broken; there are no ties. Unworldized, she can go anywhere, and the severity of her pain out there in the dark is a measure of the cost not only of having left but also of going back.

Interview with Todd Haynes |

Distillation of three phone interviews conducted by the author on November 3 and 22, 2011, and April 17, 2012.

ROB WHITE: What is your family background?

TODD HAYNES: My mom, Sherry Lynne Haynes, came from a middle-class Jewish family in Los Angeles. Her father, Arnold Semler, whom I called Bompi, and mother, Blessing, whom I called Monna, were a very supportive aspect of my upbringing. Bompi had worked in Warner Bros., starting as a messenger boy, becoming head of set construction. He was a union organizer and was close to many of the blacklisted figures in midcentury Hollywood. He left the studio in the later 1940s and set up a private business with his brother, making radio-communications devices for the military. He became very successful in the 1950s and '60s. Monna studied harp and piano, and then when she was about fifty started painting in an abstract expressionist style. She was very progressive, went into psychoanalysis in the 1950s, and continued to explore various kinds of therapies—from transcendental meditation to Rolfing to Reichian therapy. She was a sort of spiritual trailblazer. My grandparents practiced Judaism, but Monna also undertook a very modern, Californian quest for spiritual meaning and psychic growth that influenced us all. My grandparents also introduced me to concerts, films, plays, and exhibitions in L.A. They took me to New York City and Washington, D.C., when I was nine, and then to the Far East when I was fourteen, and these were extraordinary opportunities. Bompi would be one of the strongest advocates of my work. He invested money in *Poison,* and it was probably one of the proudest moments of my life to write him a check for $184,000 that returned all of his money with profits after the fairly respectable debut of that film theatrically.

My mom studied acting as a teenager, and then studied art as well. My parents were nineteen when they married. She met my dad, Allen Haynes, who wasn't Jewish, at a camp where they were both working as counselors. He had lost his father when he was seven, and his mother remarried a much older man whom he was never very close to. He had a very independent life as a teenager, involved in a radio station in college, and had a really outgoing personality. He served in the military around the time I was born in 1961. He was never posted to bases outside the U.S., but he was away from home a lot of the time. My sister Wendy was born in 1964, and she was my companion growing up—and the star of my after-dinner productions—and someone I've stayed really close to. She discovered Portland, Oregon, in her young adulthood and settled down here, and when I followed her in 2000 it ushered in a whole new adult relationship with her, which has been great. My brother Shawn was born in 1971. We all lived in the San Fernando Valley in Los Angeles and moved from smaller homes to a house that they built themselves in the early 1970s, where my dad still lives. He became a sales rep for a company which sold things like perfume atomizers. Later my brother would follow our dad and start his own cosmetics company, Girl Cosmetics, in the 1990s.

I attended public schools through elementary and junior high, and then in ninth grade I switched to a private school called the Oakwood School that was in some ways inspired by the Summerhill theories of the open curriculum. It had a progressive, even hippieish reputation, though it has become much more academically demanding. Oakwood always maintained a strong focus on the arts, and I enjoyed its smaller, attentive environment. Also, it drew a lot of kids from the entertainment industry—kids whose parents were actors or in the film business, some of whom would become actors themselves. Many of my friendships were with kids who would become actors. Elizabeth McGovern was my closest friend in high school; we did a lot of productions, plays, and performance pieces of our own—original things and adaptations—and were known for that at school. I had always been interested in painting and art-making since a young age, and that carried through to college, where I continued to paint.

RW: *Dottie Gets Spanked* was based on your own childhood?

TH: Yes. Some of my own childhood artworks can be seen in that film, including the little book about Julie Andrews and Dottie (of course, it was Lucille Ball originally). Both my parents encouraged my art-making, but my interest in fairy tales, Disney films, Julie Andrews, and Elizabeth Montgomery on television in *Bewitched* created some tension between myself and my parents, which I could absolutely feel. I remember that my favorite thing would be to go to the market with my mom, and my most coveted object would always be a drawing pad—"Can I get a pad, can I get a pad?"—and I remember once she said, "I'll buy you one if you don't only draw women." I was spanked three times, I think, by my dad. It broke with my mom's dictate that spanking was not acceptable, but in my dad's moments of temper and frustration with me, he broke down and reverted to what was practiced in his household, which wasn't progressive like my mom's. We felt that there was a sort of privileged family background, and it was my mom's, and that was the one we were exposed to and most closely intertwined with.

Realizing I was gay was unexpected, as I think it always is in one way or another. I had various dalliances and crushes in high school, but it wasn't until college when I actually had a first boyfriend that I felt I could come out. I began talking about bisexuality, in the way that people who are starting to come out try to break the ice. I was probably least worried about coming out to my mom, but as it turned out she had a kind of symptomatic meltdown and a process of examining her own culpability. It was my dad who assured me that it was alright with him. He said something to the effect of, "You know, Todd, when I was twelve I had feelings for a friend of mine that were similar, and you've just always been more intense than me, and so I can see how you would play this out more intensely in your life." It meant so much to me that he completely and totally personalized it that way. He made sure I knew he understood from a personal perspective and from his own experience. My grandparents were extremely supportive and sweet about it as well, and my brother, who was nine or ten, said, "That's cool." It was surprising that it was my mom who had the most trouble with it initially. Later she would say that my being gay taught her more, made her grow as a person, and rethink the world—that it was one of the precipitating events of her own growth and maturity. She eventually became very involved in AIDS issues in L.A. and became very close friends with gay men she would meet. So she really came full circle.

RW: You famously studied semiotics at Brown.

TH: I decided to take a year off before I started college. I saved up some money and traveled in Europe with a backpack. Also my uncles were opening up a restaurant in Hawaii, on the island of Kauai, and the first place I ever lived completely on my own after leaving home was a tiny little shack near this restaurant, which I helped build and then worked in as a busboy. For three months I lived on my own, painted constantly, listened to music, read books that I knew were going to be on some of the courses I would be taking at Brown, including Virginia Woolf and James Joyce. So I had this little moment of really rich self-education, of creative and intellectual immersion, while being independent for the first time, but away from people my own age.

By the time I went to Brown I was really ready to work. I was pretty serious-minded and applied myself to things I already knew I was interested in. Brown still had the open curriculum from the 1960s: you could construct your own concentration and majors, and so I completely embraced art, theory, and literature. Semiotics was just a program at the time, a renegade annex to the more traditional English department. Semiotics enjoyed a kind of radical, alternative status in Brown during those years. It was 1981 when I started, only just a few years after some of the seminal writing, particularly cutting-edge feminist film theory, had first come on the scene, but it was already incorporated in the program. I found myself identifying and relating quite closely. Professors like Mary-Anne Doane, in particular, and Michael Silverman, who was head of the program, became real allies and guides through that experience, and I remain in touch with them today.

I got to know Christine Vachon, producer of my films, in college. We were the same age, but I had taken that first year off, and then I took another year off in the middle as well: I felt like this was too special and unique an opportunity, and as soon as it became routine I took a break and then came back. So Christine graduated two years before me and was already in New York. She had a gig at Cable View, one of the early cable film networks, and I got a job there and then worked in galleries in SoHo as a preparator, and it was during that time that I started to work on *Superstar*. Barry Ellsworth, who was another close friend of mine and Christine's from Brown, used some family money to start a nonprofit organization, which he brought me and Christine into. That became Apparatus Productions. We filed for 501(c)(3) status and sought out grants. We got money from the National Endowment for the Arts and from the New York State Council for the Arts, and we basically helped to finance and produce what we called "experimental narrative" films. Our work with Apparatus put us in touch with a creative community in the city.

In New York I got involved with ACT UP after poster activism started to make a huge impression on me, especially the "Silence = Death" campaign. I found out where this was coming from: a new organization that was thrown together under the auspices of Larry Kramer. It was a powerful experience, to say the least. Attending those meetings meant connecting to men and women of every color and age—a lot came from the civil rights era and were now applying their experience to this new crisis. Within the larger group we started Gran Fury, made up of artists who wanted to devise visual and graphic campaigns for ACT UP. We had a New Museum exhibition that I participated in. In this work, we wanted to become our own professionals—which was one of the real mantras of ACT UP. This campaigning altered the politics around AIDS, and that was a really amazing experience for me.

RW: Beginning with *Assassins*, your films alternate between stories about rebellious queer artists and stories about trapped women.

TH: I definitely alternate, though it's not by design so much as some instinct that splits me into these opposing fields. *Superstar* contains elements of both, and maybe even this early Super 8 film that I did in high school, called *The Suicide.* It was a two-year endeavor starting in ninth grade that came out of an essay I had written for a test in humanities at Oakwood. I teamed up with a classmate, Joel Berkowitz, who was more interested in the technical aspects of filmmaking. I wrote the script based on the story, we shot it in school with friends (and even a local TV actress), but the postproduction took two years. We transferred Super 8 sound mag to 16mm sound mag, and then eventually because we were friends with Mike Martin, who was the TV producer Quinn Martin's son, moved up to 35mm sound mag and managed to get a sound mix done at Samuel Goldwyn Studios through the influence of Mike. Which meant that in 1978 we had a Super 8 projector linked up to a twenty-four-track, 35mm sound-mixing room. And, by the way, I was sort of working out my own amorous ambivalent feelings toward Joel. With *The Suicide,* we did our best to professionalize the filmmaking process—we had a miniature crew, including a script girl, the whole hierarchy—and for the premiere we even got a theater somehow in the West Village, and somebody rented us a limo to pick us up and take us there.

We had studied the hero myth that year, and I wrote my essay on the topic with black, red, and blue pens plus a pencil, splitting the voices of this discourse into the different colors. The story's through-line was about a troubled little kid who was making his transition from junior high to high school—a very sensitive kid, very fearful of that transition, and the way that he conducts a lot of the anxieties and fears is through a fantasy of killing himself. Pointedly, for somebody who would end up becoming a filmmaker, the description of this act was: "I carefully and instantly began cutting myself into several pieces." The suicide in the film is this sort of fantasy, shot through Vaseline in an all-white bathroom, involving a series of images of the boy cutting himself with scissors. But the original essay itself was also in pieces, with these various fragments of different voices allotted to different parts of his life and memories being in different colors. And the sections got shorter and shorter and more intertwined as the piece unfolded, so it anticipates some of the structural things I would later explore in a film like *Poison,* which inter-weaves three stories. But it also in a strange way embodies both a kind of repressed subject in a domestic experience (although going through very universal rites of passage in his young life) and a kind of poetic and creative—and burgeoning queer—identity that's expressed in the idea of reconstructing his life and his story in this way. So it's funny because it was obviously done very instinctively and intuitively at that age.

By the end of the whole experience of making *The Suicide*, which was as much an emotional journey through the complexities of young love and pain and all that stuff as it was a creative filmmaking experience, I felt the need to turn away from any kind of filmmaking that emulated the studio system (as our tentative little film had done). So when I went to Brown, I looked more toward experimental models. I felt that there was something to be learned from a more hands-on approach to film-making, and it wasn't until I made *Assassins* at Brown—which was again a thesis project, involving Barry Ellsworth who shot it with me (and we also had a complicated personal relationship at the time)—that I started again to work with a small crew.

Assassins was an experimental film, but it drew from narrative traditions. I was captivated by the propelling force of Rimbaud's language, but I was also extremely interested in the way that so many other artists felt that too. Rimbaud generated such identification and constant comparison to others' emergence as artists. You go to the library, and there's just a small collection of original works, and then masses of writing about him, much of which, like Henry Miller's *The Time of the Assassins,* involves famous writers placing their own life and experience alongside Rimbaud's and using him as a sort of touchstone for their own comprehension of their own emerging voices. So my film is layered with these references to other artists that frame or reframe these vignettes of Rimbaud's life. I was also interested in the whole act of translation, which reaches a peak in the sound track at the end of the film, where a passage from *Illuminations* is multiply mixed with many different English translations of the same poem and the original French version, all ringing out over each other. So the whole endeavor of trying to find Rimbaud as a subject is something that's uncertain, maybe impossible, but perhaps for exactly that reason generates tremendous desire.

RW: It's interesting that the idea of suicide was there right at the beginning. Did the sense of subjective crisis emerge from your personal experience?

TH: I think my own experience was, on the one hand, very much like any adolescent's, and particularly any emerging gay person's as we kind of leave the cocoon of the family. It was that crucial, uncertain time of trying to come to terms with who one is, around and amid and against cultural and social definitions that we are entering into, and surrounding ourselves by. Because I enjoyed a very supportive family environment that encouraged my creative interests I was left with confidence, with a sense of self-motivated assuredness in high school and in college. At the same time, I always found myself feeling identification with outcast, fragile, vulnerable people in the classroom. I had friendships with them of a more private kind—though within the bounds of a pretty comfortable, middle-class Los Angeles milieu where we weren't confronting the most challenged parts of the society. I felt a connection with, or empathy toward, kids who had a harder time fitting in, and I think that's reflected in a lot of subjects of my films and the kinds of stories I tend to tell, especially with female characters. And Lenny, the little boy in *The Suicide,* is one of these outsiders. It really wasn't my own story. But the ways that the story drew on, and the film itself drew on, creative practice to muscle through pain and difficulty in these adolescent scenarios does of course say a great deal about who I am.

I was always astounded when kids a year ahead of me in grade school had this ability to talk back to adults or even older kids. I was just not emboldened that way and was sort of shocked by other kids who were. There was definitely something mild or meek about the way I expressed my strengths and abilities—and that actually made people want to be friends with me. I still felt when it came to telling stories, I wasn't interested in telling the heroic ones. Even the artistic subjects that I would end up taking on were people who were putting themselves through various kinds of exercises in derangement of the senses, in Rimbaud's case, or Genet's identification with outcasts and with homosexuality as a criminal practice. These were artists who were rejecting the rewards and privileges that they could very easily, given their abilities and skills, have had full access to. I gravitated toward that. And all along, obviously, these are stories about artists and people who were rejecting solid, stable notions of identity and of privilege in the world.

RW: But doesn't the rejection of identity also lead to psychic meltdown—like what's experienced by Karen in the apartment scene in *Superstar?*

TH: I think there's a curiosity in my films about subjects who gravitate toward various forms of self-destruction, at various levels of consciousness, and in the case of *Superstar* you can't help but see it as related to creative success: the cost of pop-cultural visibility, the cruelty of fame, and, particularly in Karen Carpenter's case, in the years just coming out of adolescence, being thrust in the public eye at that age as a body, as a woman, and scrutinized as a result, with all the ensuing insecurity and self-ambivalence in the form of anorexia. But that visibility is coupled with this intense desire for perfection, the crazy drive of anorexia to perfect and control instincts and urges. The feeling of mastery and the high that characterizes that syndrome was so fascinating to me because it's actually still describing self-destruction (in Karen's case, total self-destruction in the end). The scene you refer to is an example of the kind of unraveling of that sense of control in the binge-purge dichotomy that defines the bulimic sensibility: indulgence, then complete, flagellant denial and self-punishment. I don't know if that particular cycle describes me personally, but I found within it the pathologies and transgressions that are a necessary component of suburban identity and existence. Those kinds of things only get worse when the suburban fantasies and dreams are forced into the public eye, under the spotlight of fame, and the pressures and the visibility get intensified. The underside of all that—the questioning, the uncertainty, the self-ambivalence if not self-destructiveness and self-hatred—becomes way more intense and life-threatening as a result.

RW: There's the amazing image of Karen sitting at the table with the *Partridge Family* clip behind her taking up the whole background, and it's like the whole side of the building has been ripped off.

TH: The scene depicts the corrosive power of mass media and the way in which the privileged white, suburban, middle-class identity that we're meant to embrace and covet in our lives is poisonous, invasive—these specters or phantoms of how to live and who to be that all the intellect and theoretical armor in the world doesn't completely protect us from. It runs through the bloodstream.

When I encountered critical theory, feminist theory, and queer theory at Brown, they felt like extensions of critical positions that I'd already experienced in my life and had begun to find ways of articulating. I discovered a whole different history and mode of expression in the theoretical discourses. And at a certain point—I was also doing some abstract painting at this time—I felt like it was a cop-out to not engage with my own ambivalence about representation, meaning, identity, images of masculinity and femininity and homosexuality, and all these burdens that we carry. I realized that the representational culture that I grew up in the midst of in Los Angeles was poisonous, coercive—I couldn't just reject or escape from it. I wanted to engage. I therefore decided, grudgingly, to take on representation and narrative in order to describe my own ambivalence. Narrative involves a relationship that can blindly reiterate or reproduce pleasure, can affirm and rebuild dominant systems of representation and meaning. But there's also the option of using those same tropes that we all know from the inside out to possibly, ideally, or potentially reveal these things—to intervene and provide barriers, obstacles, and interesting exposure to them.

I didn't think of myself as this feature-filmmaker person. I never thought that's how my career would develop. I looked at experimental filmmakers whom I encountered, like Leslie Thornton, who was just coming to Brown to teach film production at the time, and figured that that would be the way I would do it as well. I would get an MFA. I would make films that were purely experimental, but I would live as a teacher, under an academic umbrella, as a way of sustaining myself. It was through a sort of series of accidents, starting with *Superstar,* that my films found audiences. There were very specific, and I would say fortuitous, circumstances. This was particularly the case with *Poison,* which positioned me as a New Queer filmmaker, with a queer audience expecting a product that I could deliver.

RW: Were you always happy with the New Queer Cinema label?

TH: That mantle identified a group of films and filmmakers who were responding to the AIDS crisis, but with a great deal of stylistic independence and opposition to norms. I felt very lucky to be able to be a feature filmmaker at that time, with a great deal of creative freedom—and indeed defined by creative freedom to deal with these subjects. A group of people responded creatively as well as politically to a crisis (all the myriad social and cultural complexities and the panic around AIDS) in ways that are very rare in the history of film. That in and of itself was important. I felt too that I shared a desire for stylistic experimentation with the other filmmakers, and that was as exciting to me as the content.

New Queer Cinema also defined a market, though one that had always existed (the art-cinema market had always been largely gay), and films about gay people (usually gay men) wouldn't have been possible without this art-film audience. But to a large degree, these were films based on theater, or they were more traditional, tragic coming-out stories—*Boys in the Band* or *Bent* or *Fortune and Men's Eyes*—and weren't necessarily expanding the language of cinema itself. But the New Queer Cinema films and filmmakers were. I felt proud to be part of that group of filmmakers at that particular time, but I felt that the form and style mattered more than the market. How one sees the world should define queerness rather than content (and rather than how many hot guys you could have in your movie).

RW: Would you agree that Graves and Nancy in the "Horror" story of *Poison* are unexpectedly the closest you come in your films to depicting a happy couple?

TH: I like that idea. There's that romance of the utter outcasts and the mutually infected and excluded and abject. They are exceptions and markers of the other side to society and its norms. Thus there's the link to that beautiful scene in *Fear Eats the Soul* when Emmi and Ali are sitting having lunch in the restaurant that Hitler used to go to, and it's this very special moment for them, and they become the subject of the classic Fassbinderian melodramatic stares from society, glaring at their transgressive relationship crossing race and age norms—and it just makes that scene probably the most heartbreaking, touching, romantic scene in all of Fassbinder. (In *Poison,* that scene is mirrored in that more ironic, grotesque, humorous scene of Graves dripping pus into his hot dog.)

RW: Does romantic failure haunt your films?

TH: I would say in the most general sense that that's true of all great love stories, that they always end in tragedy—the best love stories always leave you desiring a different outcome. "If only" haunts the classic genre of the love story and also a sense of the lost moment, lost potential.

The other thought that came to mind when you said that was that I think I learned that something happens when you lower expectations in an audience. Real surprises can occur. I learned this first in *Superstar,* where the possibility of emotional connection to the characters seems completely absurd at the beginning of that film, given the fact that it's told with dolls. And it's about Karen Carpenter and about this music that we think we're so superior to; we know too well how manipulative that music is and how plastic and unreal, and so we're so unsuspecting of a true emotional connection that we're in the best possible place to receive one. That was definitely the goal of *Superstar,* but it's also why I think it succeeds as a film. It really is so affecting emotionally, and you don't see it coming. I think that may very well be true for the ways in which some of the stories in *Poison* don't telegraph where they're going, and what surprising emotions could come up in the process.

RW: "Homo" seems to me to downplay the edginess of Genet. Was that intended?

TH: No, that wasn't my mission. We who were involved in the activist culture of the AIDS epidemic knew that it felt great to go out and protest. What was extraordinary about those protests (as we saw recently with Occupy protests) is how successful they can be when they're specific and site-specific. We used to target specific issues literally each day: protesting in front of Burroughs Wellcome until they reduced the price of AZT and the dosage, for example. And they did. It was amazing how effective that kind of organizing can be. (Not to say that larger, messier, and more pervasively symbolic protests such as happened in '68 aren't essential and necessary—and maybe the Occupy movement is more in that line.)

Yet at the same time, what was missing also was a place to mourn the fact that we were losing so many people so fast. The horror, pain, and tragedy of that were too overwhelming. There wasn't a lot of mental space to comprehend it all. I remember Douglas Crimp writing a beautiful thing about mourning, and all of us being taken aback by this huge reservoir of feeling that we had been putting aside. I think that a sense of mourning pervades *Poison,* and other films. It's appropriate that in film, and through a narrative experience, and maybe even more through one that's allegorical, one can find room to really feel the losses that we're talking about. *Poison* is permeated by intense romantic loss, but it was also a film that I perceived as a way of intervening in the sense of self-blame that a lot of gay people were being forced to feel about their sexuality in the 1970s that preceded AIDS, and their own part in bringing it on. I felt Genet would have something really strong to say to the situation. I wanted to bridge the gap between what was happening right now and what might have been said or posed by Genet, who was never interested in trying to find a way to please or find acceptance by dominant culture or mainstream heteronormativity in any sense.

He found all of his theoretical, critical, and political inspiration from being outcast. And he clung to that dark, beautiful, and sort of sacred criminal-outsider status of the homosexual. So there's romance in that as well that I feel I was probably summoning more than the themes of total betrayal—the harder, colder aspects of his world that are in a film like *Querelle*.

RW: "Hero" is quite funny. Everybody is so exasperated by Richie's mischief, and that erases any sense that he's a victim.

TH: Also I felt it was a useful generic inclusion in the trilogy to have a sort of tabloid documentary format where the subject is missing and absent. So "Hero" also became this toggle position that the other two stories could fit in and out of—so you could more easily apply themes and aspects of the other two characters, Broom and Graves, to the Richie story. But there's definitely humor. These testimonies are funny and strange, especially because this boy was both a victim and a conductor of scenarios. He had an active presence, and he was a creator of stories and fantasies, sexual or sadomasochistic scenarios that he wanted to inflict on others. So in many ways it also made the witnesses into victims of his agenda that was never completely clear, though you could glean aspects of what it meant from the other stories in the process. But I liked that play of his coerciveness over them as well.

RW: Why is the last shot of "Hero" so moving?

TH: I don't even know. It moves me too, but for me it's mixed up with all kinds of things when I watch it now—especially how much *Poison* was, and has only become more so, a love poem to Jim Lyons. I was falling in love with him while moving into production on the film, and I wanted him to play the part of Bolton. He only agreed to do it if he could cut the movie too. So Jim's part in it all is multiplicitous and all over it and profound.

Of course, there's also a connection to Genet's treatment of childhood. At some level I identified with and saw aspects of my own childhood perversities, my own exceptionalisms, and my own childhood superpowers reflected in those ideas, but as always with Genet, I felt challenged by what I was reading and thinking, and whatever ways I felt I could find myself in his work, I always found the limits of my own middle-classness. Genet and Rimbaud were emblems and markers of extremity that challenge the ways we succumb to the rewards of society and the creature comforts of bourgeois life. I found their positions, particularly in terms of standing outside society as a gay person, particularly empowering and instructive. And I still do.

RW: In *Dottie Gets Spanked* you depict a family that, for all its difficulties, is loving—and yet there's no room in it for Stevie's sexuality. To what extent have you always been going along with an anti-nuclear-family critique, especially when it comes to the repression of homosexuality?

TH: I guess I have to say that the answer is there in the film. The best thing I can probably do is put it in the work itself. But I remember that after *Poison* and *Safe* had come out, there was an article that was put up about me at Oakwood. My brother also went to the school, and my parents stayed connected to the school years after I was there. So there was an article put up about Todd Haynes, the openly gay filmmaker and winner of the Sundance prize and so on, and I got this letter from a kid who was starting to tell me how he thinks he's probably gay and that I was out there as this gay filmmaker, and he tells me that he's in love with his best friend but could never tell him and all this stuff. Halfway through the letter, there's a break in it, and he writes: "Oh my God, this letter was on my typewriter when my mom was in the room and read it, and we had a family talk and my mother said, 'I love you, and I accept you for who you are,' and my dad said, 'I love you, and I accept you for who you are, and you'll always be my son,' and I told my girlfriends at school, and they said, 'That's so cool that you're gay,' and I told my best friend who I'm in love with, and he said, 'That's really cool, man. I love you as a friend'"—and then he said: "I'm in so much pain, and it's so awful, and I don't know what to do"! And you realize that even when you're in the most perfect conditions and your culture is there to meet you and there's *Will and Grace* on TV and there's Todd Haynes on your bulletin board at school, or whatever it is, and your best friend is saying "I love you, man," you still know the coded meaning of life in your world. You know what the heterosexual culture instills.

Yet I also suspect that there's this element of feeling not right in everybody when they come into being who they are, but when you're gay it's more so, and when you're black it's more so. The society is telling you that if you do these things you're gonna be fine, and everything's good, and you'll be accepted, but you never really believe it, and you never really feel it, and we're haunted by that. That was what was so brilliant about Hitchcock: he found the most universal uncertainty about our own sense of being guilty. He tapped into the fact that we are always all guilty, and it can just be triggered by the smallest thing. A man is suspected of the murder, and even though he's the wrong man, he feels culpable and completely and totally wrong, guilty, susceptible, and poisoned.

So I just found that letter to be so remarkable. It was a different set of circumstances that this kid was coming out of than I had, and yet mine were ideal compared to so many people's. I just don't have this idea that it's ever perfect and that society can just roll out the red carpet for every person's sense of who they are coming into the world.

RW: There's an extremely pronounced sense of alienation in *Safe,* too.

TH: I really did feel that *Safe* was as much a product of the AIDS culture and my own questions about how illness and how AIDS in particular were being interpreted—and how those interpretations were being foisted on people who were sick, who now had to carry a further burden of culpability for their illness. In both *Poison* and *Safe,* I thought that the largest, most interesting, and most enduring themes that AIDS was bringing up could be best described through allegory and through a broader recourse to narrative traditions. The issues could then be looked at from a longer view, with a through-line that encompassed more of American society and American films.

In terms of visual style and narrative style, I was thinking of films that had an icy, controlled, restrained template like Kubrick's. I wanted to convey what it felt like to be in modern airports and controlled environments, and of course I was thinking a lot about my own experience where my parents ended up—up in the hills of Los Angeles, among these new homes and wealthy facades. I was also trying to come to grips with people I'd met in that world through family members and friends of family who I really felt an incredible distance from, people I felt I could never come to really understand. I made a concerted effort to put one of those people at the center of this story as a way of finding my way to them. As I mentioned, the intense need that a viewer has to identify and fill meaning into anything that they're given in a film is so interesting to me. As with *Superstar,* in *Safe* I put up barriers that viewers were bound to circumvent.

What interested me in *Safe* was how somebody could reach an ultimate place and become almost politicized, or brought to a sense of consciousness, when they found themselves completely at odds with—constitutionally just in opposition to—their environment and who they thought they were supposed to be. This paradigm or parable of environmental illness could have seemed like just a made-up illness or like a completely philosophical proposition. The idea of becoming allergic to the twentieth century, becoming physically incapable of existing in these dream states and this manufactured world, seemed like the perfect pretext for this story I wanted to tell. And then watching the industries of recovery do their work to sort of re-tamp-down a person into their codified meaning and back into a sense of identity that had been lost, that had been ruptured by the process. I was interested in the Louise Hay stuff—the ways in which people with HIV were being instructed to take back control over their situations and feel in control of their illnesses by learning how to love themselves again because it was that lack of love for themselves that had gotten them in this state. There was a curiously cruel double message in that—the way we so seek to feel in control of ourselves and our lives, and how illness can so upset that, and how we search for narratives to tell us how we got sick and why it was our fault. Like when a kid's parents get divorced, the only way the kid can understand it is that it's something they did. We opt out and elect to be culpable for things as a way of finding meaning and control over them. I just found that to be such a poignant and universal response.

It's the before and the after that are the repressive sides of the story. The point of a sort of radical hope is in the middle of the film. That's where Carol might actually learn something and make a change in her life for the better—and revolt. Her body is already in revolt. The moments of hope are few and far between. It's just her feeling completely abject and incompatible with her own life and everything that marks familiar territory for her and who she's supposed to be and who she always thought she was. All of those things feel so paper-thin ultimately in this film. All of the ways that we feel the opposite in stories—the way we feel that characters are solid and reliable and follow generic traditions and tropes—are in many ways just as constructed and just as paper-thin and just as much the product of conventions and expectations and our own filling-in as viewers, and that's true of *Safe* as well. I tried to have somebody so incredibly unheroic at the core of it, and somebody whose voice was so thin and whose body becomes as thin and translucent as her identity. Then there's a series of breakdowns and things beginning to become undone. It's the middle that's the hopeful part of the film (within the very tenuous and consistent fragility and sort of house of straw that's set up as the storyline and as cues to her interiority, which are so fragile and so uncertain).

In the middle everything is completely falling apart, and in a way she doesn't even know who she is anymore. But maybe that's the beginning of something potentially great. Instead she's told exactly who she is by this whole new industry of meaning and identity. The film also follows the formal conventions and expectations that we know from the disease movie of the week: characters come to learn about their illness, and since often these illnesses are not curable, the resolution of these stories is more about a coming to an acceptance and a sense of knowing oneself through illness and joining with other sufferers of that illness. That's supposed to be the narrative reward of these films, and *Safe* gives you that—but it's the wrong answer.

RW: So before Carol goes to Wrenwood, there's a possibility that she could let herself be unmade by this world she can't deal with and isn't even going to fight against—and this process could have had some outcome other than Wrenwood, an outcome that might have been positive and transformative?

TH: Yeah—and even her scene with the other women with environmental illness, all saying about how you can't go anywhere anymore and almost laughing, and there's even a groupthink. Joining that group of people is stepping out of anything that's known to her, and it also feels like she's dealing with people of different classes and races.

Just everything is new and different. All of a sudden every smell, every color, every texture in her world is potentially dangerous and lethal. That experience could be politicizing because you're looking at the dangers of the everyday and the dangers of what we're supposed to think of as happy norms that actually are pollutants and essentially destructive devices. Or when Carol stands up to the doctor and says, "It's the chemicals." What she's calling the cause is just scratching the surface of an overall critique of middle-class life and its rewards system and its system of privilege that other people have criticized in a lot of different ways, and for all the right reasons, and especially in terms of what it might do to women in particular and their own sense of who they are within this world as trophies for men and emblems of success, and just one more of the shiny objects accrued to define success in the world—all of these things that are no longer possible for Carol in this middle phase of her life and the middle phase of the story. But it's brief.

RW: Do you see any connection between your films and post-punk music, which was often more melodic and mournful than punk?

TH: I think it was all in the air: I think there was a way in which indie film and experimental film were informing New York post-punk bands like Sonic Youth. I know that they saw *Superstar,* and they were very interested in that film and its approach. That was one of the precursors to us working together on my one rock video, for their *Goo* record, "Disappearer," and on that record was their tribute to Karen, "Tunic," and I think it was another part of a countercultural reassessment of pop-cultural iconography and sentiment that found a new way of connecting back to the past with surprising results. That was true for *Superstar* and for a lot of the Sonic Youth work that came out at that time. When I would visit my folks in Los Angeles and was starting to consider the ideas and strategies for *Safe,* I would just drive away from their house in the car and sit alone and smoke and listen to Sonic Youth and look at the facades of these houses. Their music and sensibility inspired me in ways that weren't necessarily manifesting themselves in the specific films but were really inspirational nonetheless.

At the same time, though, experimental films were also beginning to reincorporate narrative, genre, and emotion, and that was something that definitely was a turning point for me, Christine, Barry, and people I was working with coming out of college in terms of what the future of counterproduction in film might look like. *Thriller,* Sally Potter's blend of experimental and genre traditions, was very important to us, and at a more mainstream point on the spectrum I remember feeling kinship when I went to see *Blue Velvet.* There was again a kind of incorporation of ironic positions around discarded generic styles, but without denying emotional access. There was a complicated, interesting, humorous, but definitely postmodern reassessment of emotion in various forms, whether filmic or musical.

RW: You start out as an avant-garde filmmaker, then *Poison* and *Safe* are quintessential indie movies. So was *Velvet Goldmine* your entry into the more mainstream industry?

TH: You know, some of those distinctions are somewhat hard to absolutely lay down concretely. In many ways, I feel like a line can be drawn between *Poison* and *Safe,* and that *Poison* was financed fully through arts grants and felt very much outside the machinery and the financing world of feature filmmaking, whereas *Safe* wasn't, and we thoroughly exhausted all the various options of financing for that film. It took several years to get it made, but it really was film money—American Playhouse helped get that film made—and it was shot in L.A. Of course, it was a low-budget crew—the people who work on porn by day and then low-budget indie film at night (or vice versa)—but it was still like we were making a movie in L.A. with professional crews and a professional film production. *Velvet Goldmine* was just all the more ambitious a project, and it necessitated shooting in London and getting to know that system, but each film had a slightly bigger budget than the last and different sets of expectations going in. And I was working with more name actors as well in *Velvet Goldmine.* So each of them was a step into official film production.

With *Velvet Goldmine,* I wanted to make a film that really rekindled the spirit of late 1960s and early '70s filmmaking—the culture that produced glam rock and was a hybrid of various unexpected influences crossing each other, as in the Chelsea, London milieu, where the underworld was mixing with the avant-garde, rock 'n' roll, and gay cultures, and producing certain kinds of art and music. It was also producing film as well—and *Performance* became a seminal point of reference for *Velvet Goldmine* stylistically, but also almost in a spiritual sense. That film and others at the time came out of drug culture. At this interestingly mobile, mutable time, a kind of cinema emerged that meant a great deal to a teenager like myself: I could enter a world that one had to interpret and revisit. Kubrick's *2001* and *A Clockwork Orange* played a real part in that fantasy world. These films became almost like planetary objects that you would enter, reenter, analyze, and continue to peel the layers off. This generated an intense fan relationship to these dream films and rock 'n' roll drug movies. The glam-rock experience and idea were so based on the kinds of possibility and cross-sections of influence that were generating at this time that I really felt it made total sense to move into that realm. This also relates to how the sound track evolved in marrying people of the time with contemporary musicians.

RW: You talk in your preface to the Barney Hoskyns *Glam!* book about that early-1980s moment when David Bowie and Lou Reed renounced their supposedly gay identities, and I wondered which of the male characters (if any) in *Velvet Goldmine* are meant to be gay in a lasting way.

TH: The thing about *Velvet Goldmine* and that whole period is that these kinds of questions about who's gay and who's straight are meaningless. I loved that period and found it to be radical, and continue to feel that way about it, because there were no secure identity politics. This was probably why it wasn't a film that was as embraced by the gay community as I would have hoped—there wasn't a clear-cut evocation of gay identity in *Velvet Goldmine.*

Glam blurred sexual orientations, masculinity and femininity, English music and American music, dandy music-hall influences of English culture and the hard-rock world of American post-hippie music. It was the gray area that inspired simultaneous rejections of the authenticity of rock 'n' roll and the authenticity of self-expression. Instead it elevated theatricality, performance, identification with science fiction and space culture. This is why glam makes so much sense to adolescence, which is a period of indeterminacy and searching to find who you are. This sort of offering of being able to dress yourself up into who you are, and have it be a matter of costume and gesture and prerogative, is why it made so much sense to teenagers (and continues to)—and, interestingly, how much it makes sense to teenage girls, who were so drawn to the glam-rock boys. It was teenage girls who embraced *Velvet Goldmine* and became the official spokespeople for its intense fan following, which also has a slash-fiction manifestation on the Internet. There's a whole tradition in East Asia of such fiction produced by women for teenage girls but involving androgynous boys who fall in love with each other. Thus, again, any simple lines between gay/straight, male/female are blurred today also.

The slash-fiction side of it (which I think started with *Star Trek*) relates beautifully to the scene in *Velvet Goldmine* where I'm quoting myself, quoting *Superstar,* with the little girls playing with the Brian and Curt dolls under the table, then the dolls fall down out of frame like they're going to start making love. After *Velvet Goldmine* was released on DVD, we started seeing hundreds of these stories every week: best triple-X-rated story of the week, best softcore story of the week. It was an amazing creative reaction to the film, like the kind that *Mary Poppins* first generated for me—that obsessional relationship to the film that did start me into the idea of making films of my own. I don't think I've ever made a film that's generated that kind of effect on young people. I just did the commentary for the new Blu-ray edition of the film, and I went back to the fan sites—wonderful sites that have chronicled the research and the back stories behind every aspect of *Velvet Goldmine*. They're really beautiful and gorgeously annotated and intelligent, and they were a tremendous help to me to get myself back into it.

RW: I'm interested in the fluidity of gender identities when set against the sadness of where *Velvet Goldmine* ends up, the sadness of Mandy and Arthur. How much does *Velvet Goldmine* discover pain of one kind or another underneath all the flamboyancy, theatricality, and gender fluidity?

TH: I definitely felt that I wanted to explore this early 1970s pop-cultural moment. I wanted to do it with a sense—and even this sense I was taking from the language and narrative embedded in glam rock itself, and even in David Bowie's work alone—that it was all a fleeting, lost moment of possibility, and that it would all vanish through your fingers, and that the traces of it (sort of like that emerald pin that keeps moving from recipient to recipient) were also going to leave behind layers of repression and denial. Thus *Velvet Goldmine* grimly depicts a constructed and artificial 1984, one inspired to some degree by Bowie's Orwellian song "1984" but also inspired by the actual Reagan 1980s. This was the time when Bowie enjoyed his greatest success, and also when he relinquished his bisexual roots in this comic-strip character (yet another character—and there would be more to come when, I think, he started to realize that his *Serious Moonlight* success hadn't been accompanied by the critical acclaim or attention that he'd enjoyed in previous years).

I felt at the beginning of my career with *Assassins* that you can't really give the audience the revolution, and you can't give them Rimbaud. You can show the possibilities and the conditions that make one's own personal revolt or one's own personal revolution necessary, but to completely provide some answer is depriving the viewer of finding it themselves and making it their own. I sort of have it both ways in *Velvet Goldmine*: it's steeped in the sense of loss, in the barriers of repression. It's ultimately this young man Arthur's burden to deliver a story about the past that we quickly suspect has as much to do with his own past and his own relinquishing of possibilities as it does with wider histories. There's this weight and sadness in it. But even at the height of glam rock, the music had mourning and melancholy in its tone—in Roxy Music there's a sense of loss and mourning. It's not giddy, it's not hysterical, it's drenched in melancholy.

There's a sense of lost time in Arthur's past. I was obviously taking the whole idea of the *Citizen Kane* structure further. The light gets turned on the silhouetted journalist who's supposed just to be there to interview the people who knew Kane. We realize that he's actually going to be a central character, if not the central character. Arthur is us, he's me, he's the fan who's the recipient of this cultural legacy, and yet where we find him later in his life he's a drained-out, beaten-down, mere fragment of what seemed possible in that moment of youth and sexual exploration and musical discovery. The options have closed down. But it goes on: there are still those fans in the bar at the end and, yes, we wanted them to look pathetic and half-lit, but you see that every kid needs their icon, their musical crush, and this is just what they happen to have. It's a shadow, a diminished version, but it's also valid. It's a double-edged sword when it comes to revolutions that were being explored at this time. They were fleeting, and they were followed with decadence, repression, denial. If you're only looking at changing yourself, and you don't look at the world, sometimes this is what can happen.

RW: What's interesting to me about Cathy in *Far from Heaven* is that she actually seems content with normality and the security of domesticity.

TH: It's not like Carol White, who we just suspect from the start is going through the motions of who she's supposed to be: there's a gulf there, something lacking, a missing component. So it's almost like we're relieved that she develops physical symptoms that start to manifest the discrepancy between this person and her life. But Cathy embodies a perfect image of suburban contentment and those values being totally fulfilled and satisfied, and she is the attractive embodiment of all of that. But immediately there are problems. They don't seem to be rooted to her connection to herself as much as in her relationships to her husband and her children—and, of course, in the way the style is so extreme and the language so overdetermined, impenetrable. Any sense of authentic experience seems impossible, or at least almost amusing, when you're first watching *Far from Heaven.* And one can't help but watch it and be forced to think of other movies like it in the 1950s and our presumptions about that time.

Then stuff starts to happen. I always wanted it to be a story of really decent people who (like the subjects of Sirk melodramas) aren't fully equipped to deal with the big challenges of life when they are confronted with them. The characters turn out to be fragile and uncertain at their core when things aren't going right, and so it only takes a few revelations about each of these three characters—Raymond, Cathy, Frank—for each of them to take a step toward desires that, if fulfilled, would inflict unimaginable pain and conflict on the others.

I wanted *Far from Heaven* to be this pure diagram of social subjects caught in a very curtailed, very highly codified social time and place where just any step outside norms would be painful even though coming from the most honest, human places. So you couldn't really indicate a villain or culprit, and you'd have to look at the system, society, and time as the real problem. You watch these people try very hard to make it right, or go back to their original positions, and fail. You see there's no good solution, and so all three people suffer in various ways along the social spectrum of oppression around race and sexuality. Even their relative statuses are comparable but different, and, surprisingly, Frank has the most mobility because he can hide the most from the public eye and pursue his desires undercover. Even minor steps by Raymond—just touching Cathy in public—completely ricochet. And ultimately she's at the bottom rung of the hierarchy; she's the one burdened with maintaining the social structure and the family structure. In the end she has the least freedom because of that.

RW: But wouldn't you say also the least desire for freedom? Isn't there something about Cathy that she's never going to break out? Isn't she, unlike Carol, safe?

TH: That's interesting, and I think it's true to some degree. Except that I don't know that she's ever safe again once she develops an affection for Raymond. I think that changes the climate and the temperature of her life. But that isn't to say that possibly it could never have happened, and Frank would have always desired Cathy, and they would have been fine. Everybody's experience triggers a discovery in everybody else, and they learn something. I think Cathy discovers an incompatibility with what she thought was just fine. I think that's more the result. In her gut she has all the right instincts toward how to deal with African Americans, but there's a tenderness and a vulnerability that gets shared between them, and she can't go back from that.

RW: And Raymond?

TH: I definitely remember wanting to contrast an etiquette around race with more insidious or shocking examples of contradictory feelings about race. But even more than that, I was thinking about the liberal tradition of depicting the idealized black subject in movies. I was consciously trying to force us to look at liberal good intentions. This tradition isn't demeaning, but it's sort of skittish about truly entering the complex and potentially contradictory experience of a black person in America at that time. The way Cathy talks about race is good-hearted but naive. It's insufficient and fragile. The attack on Raymond's daughter and the fleeing of people from the swimming pool, and the immediate hostility—almost a chemical reaction—that occurs when he touches her in public outside the movie theater are events that cut through the congeniality. It's important that a dialectic is set up between the two modes. I always felt that we were contrasting different kinds of societal marginality, different kinds of intolerance. *Far from Heaven* forces us to examine the unfair burden of visibility that race carries versus the remarkable freedom of invisibility that a closeted gay man can enjoy. And yet these dueling social positions that are easy for us to talk about in hindsight from a more seemingly progressive time historically still both have a greater potential for self-expression than that of the woman who ultimately has to surrender.

Raymond loses a lot. He has to leave this town and start anew. His transgressions are magnified because of the burden of visibility that he carries. Race and color of skin and how the issues play out so beautifully in a film like *Imitation of Life* were always there percolating in what we tried. And the whole idea of visibility and tension between what's beneath the surface versus what's on the surface is so seminal to melodrama. It's a narrative tradition of intense visibility—it doesn't have the prerogative of tragedy to unveil truths and change a character's mind and a character's ability to mobilize in the world. People are stuck with the assigned roles and fates that society prescribes, and I find that very poignant.

RW: Can you speak about the allusions in *Far from Heaven*?

TH: I suppose there's a way that some audiences can watch *Far from Heaven* and not be aware of the films that it's referring. But even if they don't know the references, still I think because we have a distance from the characters, in a weird way the film pulls us out of the story because of its severe attention to the objects—the lighting, sets, clothes, the things that are usually meant to play a background, subsidiary role to the story and the emotion. Maybe even more than in the 1950s melodramas, these details are a distraction from the story—or at least they're being examined with a spotlight.

There are two interesting stories I'll tell about people's reception to *Far from Heaven*. I had a screening in Portland at the Cinema 21, a great single-screen old theater. It was the home screening with all my friends, and I was sitting next to this young guy who I was friends with, and he was watching the film and he was laughing along through the whole movie in recognition of the references. I didn't really mind it—it was kind of like tagging the meaning, referencing, and stitching together, almost showing the spectatorial secondary pleasure of watching the craftsmanship and all the ideas that are between us and Cathy's experience. I don't remember if it was bugging me or not at a certain point, like if it was too much. (I remember people laughing at Sirk movies in college, and there being a discussion about that—you know, the superiority that we feel toward the 1950s and the codes and manners and sexual politics of that time and our need to demonstrate that we know better.) Anyway, he was doing that little laughing thing all the way through until the scene with Cathy and Raymond outside in Raymond's back yard almost at the end of the movie—this nervous laughing, tagging—and then suddenly, when she says the line "No one would know us there," he just burst into tears. Without missing a beat, tears were just propelling from his face, projectile tears. It was instant, and I was just astounded by that switchover, how quickly it could go from self-conscious Brechtian awareness of the sources and the construction to pure emotion. I think that says so much about the melodramatic experience.

The other story is about a friend in the film world who'd never got around to seeing *Far from Heaven* until the screener came. Finally, she was home watching it with her three-year-old kid on her lap. She thought the kid was sleeping, but at the end of the movie at the train station she hears her child crying, and she says, "Honey, what's the matter? Are you okay?" And the little kid says, "Mommy, why can't that nice lady be with that nice man?" And again I just thought: wow, I can't imagine that I would ever have made a film that communicates in that most basic way, using all of the language of cinema to tell the most simple, pure story. Sort of how Hitchcock manages to do the complicated implicating of the subject in the story but using the most popular mechanisms of narrative identification and suspense—implicating you as well in the guilt of the person who is drawn into the crime or whatever it is. This is something I admire so much in Hitchcock because it's so radical and subversive and yet so mainstream and popular at the same time. Maybe this is the closest I'll come to something similar, including just seeing *Far from Heaven* get a meaty critical reception (unlike my other films) and get its Oscar nominations and have that moment in the mainstream sun. Maybe that was testament to the form and the traditions that we were stitching in and quoting from so carefully. Somehow, at a certain point, they functioned as pure emotion. That's really awesome and something I would never have necessarily expected. But I thought *Far from Heaven* was the most experimental thing I'd done to date because we were sticking so close to those conventions.

RW: It seems like there might be a link between the mournful side of glam and the weight of the past in Bob Dylan's music.

TH: I think Dylan and his universe is full of such a pantheon of instincts and energies driving him in different directions. I would say, though, that at times in the 1960s there was this sense of him being so exuberantly connected to the moment—a sense of the now, the new, and a kind of rejection of the past. But all of that built upon a concerted fascination with the traditions of folk music, the traditions of American folklore, the roots traditions that inspired Woody Guthrie (where Dylan's sense of identity first fused). But then everything that followed the peak of modernity epitomized by the Jude character played by Cate Blanchett in *I'm Not There,* and the crash-and-burn of 1966, propelled Dylan back into the past in exile from the present and away from that sense of intense urban modernity. I think in some ways he may never have left that exile, and he kind of exists in that netherland of all of these strains of the past, connecting back to musical legacies that keep him inspired and informed about what drives him but also kind of protected from the wrath of his celebrity and his presence in the world. Dylan would continue to splinter himself into different manifestations, particularly in the 1960s, which was such a dense and rapidly changing acceleration of his work and persona, but I think that was out of the need simply to protect the creative process from the expectations and demands that fame inflicted on him. There was almost a kind of aggressivity about the way he would disappoint and reject fans' expectations with each new manifestation. But it was out of a sense of basic survival, of just keeping that little flame protected from the winds of expectation and desire.

RW: In terms of the song choice in *I'm Not There,* you build up to "Idiot Wind," "I'm Not There" itself, and "Sad-Eyed Lady of the Lowlands," which are among the most expressive and the most pained of all Dylan's songs.

TH: Your description of those songs sort of says it all. They're these memorials to himself and to the phases that he's been through, starting with one that's the most about the death of a relationship. And then "Sad-Eyed Lady of the Lowlands," which is one of the most beautiful love songs—or love symphonies, given its length and breadth—ever written, but it has such an elegiac, funereal tempo and breadth to it. It feels like it's summoning up a long carnival past, the end of every carnival, the glitterdust it leaves behind, the dawn that follows as the troupe moves on to another city or another town; the song just has that sense of time being pulled across the sky that is so epic. Yet, interestingly, with all of those attributes, it's still the centerpiece of his most urbane piece of work, *Blonde on Blonde,* that feels so contemporary, urban, arch, humorous, ironic, witty, scathing, and full of a kind of cocksure energy and poetic freedom that feels very contemporary. That song starts to turn the wheels forward and backwards almost at the same time—and Dylan's career would continue like this. The fact that I was able to put that song into anything I've made, with the full approval of the artist, and to have that exquisite soliloquy of Cate's paralleling it at the end, still gives me a sense of unbelievable privilege.

When you talked about going back to the past, this summoning energy in Dylan, it reminded me that really the whole evolution of *I'm Not There* started when I began to have doubts about my life in New York and whether that was really where I wanted to continue to live and prosper as a creative person. I was having a couple of rougher years there at the very end of the 1990s, and I found myself suddenly craving Bob Dylan. I hadn't listened to his music like that since I was a teenager, and I think I was myself summoning that adolescent energy which Dylan's voice, drive, certainty epitomize better than anything. I just became obsessed with him again. It was just so symptomatic of the energy I needed to draw from my own past in order to take me somewhere else in my life and across the country. My plan was just to go to Portland to write this melodrama idea of mine, but the sound track was Dylan, and then I started reading all the biographies, and reading more and more and more, and then I bought the *Anthology of American Folk Music* halfway across that drive across country, and I bought the first bootleg series (the three-disc collection), which I found so revelatory and amazing, and it all sort of unspooled from there. It really was this revolution in my life to go to Portland, a kick in the pants in every possible way. I found myself just wanting to turn over a new leaf so much and meet new people and become newly available to the world in this new place, and that all happened while I was obsessing about Dylan and while I was watching Sirk films and writing the script for *Far from Heaven* by night. Then I basically just fell in love with the city and the great people I met there, and decided to stay. So both of those projects really were born in the energy of needing change but having to go back to my own past and my own adolescence to find it.

RW: There's all this quiet, steady business going on in *Mildred Pierce*, but also this sense of a false calm, things under the surface. Does this ambiguous mood relate to the influence of films like *Klute*?

TH: I still don't really know what *Mildred Pierce* is like to live through. It's such a different shape than anything I've made because it's a multi-part television work, which is really new to me. I didn't have the same understanding of this seemingly more open-ended form as I do with film and its generic traditions. Of course, I love the condensation that's required in genres and how experience is reduced to that hour-and-a-half experience, with all the artificial pressures that are exerted on the narrative—I find that to be one of the most interesting things about making films. This project was a step away from such formal constraints, although of course Jon Raymond and I honored the novel as much as I ever have honored a single source.

The episodes have different, even arbitrary, forms. Part 3 has a very strange temporal structure because of the leap in time. Parts 1, 2, and the first part of 3 are all set in 1931, and it's very methodical and slow as it plays out that one year. Then all of a sudden it takes this leap forward in time that it then continues to do throughout the remaining parts: 3

and 5 are the most jam-packed with events and action, communicating a lot of plot stuff that we had to shoehorn in. But part 4 ended up being this much more quiet and reflective episode that I felt we really needed between 3 and 5, returning almost to the territory of the classic domestic maternal melodrama, where the mother is trapped in the home. She's separated from the action, peeking through keyholes and waiting for Veda to come home. Veda being a teenager is where the real action lies, but it's off-camera most of the time.

Overall, though, I was really thrilled, and it was quite purposeful that I was making something for a potential audience that I'd never had before, television viewers who wouldn't be coming to *Mildred Pierce* because they were cineastes, they'd seen my last film and were curious about what I was going to do next, or that they were followers of New Queer Cinema or any of that. The audience was going to turn on the TV because Kate Winslet was on. I welcomed that. That to me was exciting and a real opportunity to actually speak in a different manner to an audience.

Stylistically, I was curious about the notion of referring to this seemingly unrelatable group of New Hollywood films, which were not for television (although the TV movie took form in the 1970s as well). These 1970s films made one feel that even if they were following their generic traditions and set in the past very often, they were somehow always talking about the present. You felt an awareness of the social-economic climate of the Watergate era in those great films. I also wanted to observe how the language of those films just sort of quieted down the directives that more stylized forms of those same genres might have given in the decades past, allowing breathing space for viewers that I felt made them feel respected—that they were sophisticated, and that they were able to locate meaning for themselves. The way the cinematographer, Gordon Willis, holds on longer, wider shots, letting action play itself out, plus the reduced editing, the naturalist performances, and the sense of natural light that permeates so many of these movies—all of this was instrumental in the way that we wanted to organize *Mildred Pierce*.

So I was trying to give the viewers at home a little space to navigate this story. At its core, the story is a fusing of emotion and economics, and it's completely about class and social standing and how that interricocheted with the mother-daughter dilemmas at home. It also felt relevant to the economic crisis that we were and are in, but also kind of universal, and talking about class in ways that few American films or stories do.

RW: Despite Winslet's amazingly sympathetic performance, there's this savagery about Mildred. In your series, do we buy Cain's idea that Mildred only loved Veda "too well" as opposed to too much?

TH: Oh God, yes. She's got pathological blinders on, and she's completely confused about the boundary of romantic love. She needs her daughter's love and approval, and it's sad. You see this amazingly able person who just has absolutely no self-awareness, and that's okay if she wasn't stuck on this daughter.

Another way to look at this is that I never wanted Monty to be a culprit. I actually think there's a kind of innocence to him. Sure, he's full of his class attitudes, and probably he does have ambivalence about the fact that Mildred works for a living and smells like grease and pays the bills. But all this is going to become so outmoded as the American middle-class sensibility unfolds with full force after the war years that you feel like they actually had a real shot, because I also felt that he was genuinely attracted to her and she was genuinely attracted to him. With just a few little adjustments, it could have been a really good relationship for her—had she not just been so primordially fixated on getting something from Veda that she was never going to get, and also never letting the poor kid go. We tried in many ways to make Veda as human and relatable a character as possible. You watch the evolution of this girl but we always tried to show Mildred's part in every aspect of that—how much was invested in this little French-speaking child, and how much that made everybody in the family feel rewarded when Veda showed off as a kid. Her musical talent, whether she really is gifted or not musically, was unfairly at the root of whether the Pierces were going to succeed as a middle-class family. Veda's abilities were going to prove whether it was all worth it or not, instead of just letting the kid off the hook so she could be what she wants to be. When Veda has her tantrum in part 4, she's being a regular teenager. To me that was the honest, universal protest any teenager under the pressure of too much mother love would make.

I wanted to really show Mildred's culpability in the development of Veda's neuroses and fixations. But it was hard because there were times in the book when Mildred just felt too calculating—especially the way when she finds out that Veda's a singer toward the end, she just literally picks up the phone and calls Monty and completely fabricates this new rekindling of a relationship with Monty to get Veda back, which makes her way more cynical than in the film. I wanted you to believe that Mildred and Monty had this genuine affection for each other, but it gets so complicated, and there are so many different motives mixed up in it all. So we just had Mildred run into Monty, a little bit more spontaneous, and there would be a feeling that this maybe could work, there's something good here, there's some real genuine history and understanding between them by this time. Mildred's blind spots were among the most interesting things in the story.

RW: And yet of all the characters in your films she gets the most gratification.

TH: Yeah, sexually and in the world of business and commerce. She's so gifted. Yet one of the things I also loved about the book from the very beginning was the way in which Mildred takes her emotional frustrations from the Veda relationship and sublimates them into work and unbelievable productivity, though even those successes always fall short, always are secondary, always are things that she can immediately give up to get what she thinks she really wants, which is Veda. But I related to that. I related to being fueled by emotional or romantic frustration at certain points in your life, or a bad relationship you're in or whatever it is, and then just seeing how you can make that into gold. You spin those frustrations into productivity and success in your work, but you're still completely captive—it doesn't help you in the end. It doesn't necessarily make you aware or change those patterns that precipitated it to begin with, so the pathologies are instrumental through the whole thing.

RW: Even though Veda's voice never abates, when Mildred stumbles away from the radio it epitomizes an extreme, sorrowful solitude that for me is a defining characteristic of your work.

TH: In that scene Mildred reactivates an intense romantic desire that functions most intensely at a distance. The scene is closely aligned to how it's described in the novel, where it's a reaffirmation of a commitment to Veda. Mildred hears that aria, that voice, and all of a sudden reconnects with the banished daughter or the daughter who's left her—the abandoned, escaped, lost daughter. After Veda leaves home, Mildred has to traverse the distance between them, becoming a prowler outside her daughter's apartment. She's now in the classic role of the unrequited lover banished from the source of her desire. The moments of the most heightened desire for Mildred happen from this distance, as when she watches Veda perform at the concert hall in episode 5. So much is rekindled when she listens to the radio—a kind of passionate determination, but based on exclusion and removal. It's a cathartic return to the desire that propels Mildred. The motivating energy that propels her machine into action is always about reaching the lost daughter. In episode 4, she has truly lost Veda. All of the discoveries she then makes about Veda's newly revealed gifts and successes as a coloratura soprano serve to reacquaint Mildred with the driving passions that fuel her, and that she has in a way lost sight of. The Mildred Pierce businesses seem almost on automatic pilot throughout most of episode 4. It's not until the crisis with Veda and the actual separation from her daughter for the first time in her life that Mildred begins to find her way back to that motivating drum beat that really gives every fiber of her abilities new meaning and purpose—to get this girl back. It's a double-sided coin, or it's a contradictory premise of the love-story genre, especially the maternal or feminine love story. What keeps two lovers separate from each other also rekindles and reinstigates the desire. It's through loss, separation, distance that we have the strongest feelings. So there's a pleasure in the pain of that exile that I think you see in that scene and elsewhere in my films as well.

RW: Twenty-seven years on from *Assassins*, what have you learned in terms of the political questions that are explored in your work and also addressed by feminism and queer theory? Do you have any answers?

TH: No! I think in a lot of ways the world has continued to just move far away from the kinds of radical questions that I felt free to ask during the feminist schooling that I enjoyed and grew from. And issues of queerness arising from activist positions against the status quo, against heternormativity in the world, were formative in the late 1980s and early '90s.

We thought Nixon was the worst it was going to get, and then it was Reagan, and then 9/11 happened, and Bush's presidency became fortified to push its most extreme foreign policy decisions and continued to stoke the social-conservative issues at home. Now the rhetorical unleashing of the far right is shocking. They brazenly can say in public the things they always kept behind closed doors and had to find all these circuitous ways of expressing or condoning. Now it's no-holds-barred, it's a free-for-all in this attack on Obama's legitimacy as president (not unlike similar attitudes toward Clinton). It's hard because I always took the New Deal for granted. I took antitrust legislation of the 1910s for granted. Now we all of a sudden have to address the most basic civil liberties and assumptions about our culture and who we are. Of course, it's great to see gays able to marry in more and more states and that becoming a more mainstream, populist presumption, but at the same time there's a loss of radicalism as a result of complete entrenchment into the mainstream. Gays in the military or gay marriage—these are the defining issues of queer communities in the West now. To stand outside and question where dominant culture is going is less and less something that young people are necessarily embracing in the way that happened when I was younger. The recent Occupy energies are extraordinary, and they're fascinating to watch—you just don't know what's going to happen and how long that movement will last and what will happen to those strains on the left as they become voiced.

I don't mean to end on such a downer, but I think the culture has taken us by surprise, and the dominance of the right and its amazing successes in attracting popular opinion are unending. So my next project is trying to look into how that has worked so well for populist sentiment in middle America, appealing to Republican and conservative policies time and again. What is that about exactly and how does that happen? It's something that's been grating on me for too long. I need to learn and get inside that a little bit more and try to actually tell a story that might even be something that people like that would go see.

The Suicide (1978)
High-school short film codirected with Joel Berkowitz
23 min.

Assassins: A Film Concerning Rimbaud (1985)
Director, Editor, Writer, and Producer: Todd Haynes
Writer and Producer: Robert Manenti
Directors of Photography: Barry Ellsworth, Todd Haynes, Robert Manenti
Cast: Bruce Cree (Rimbaud), Phelim Dolan (Verlaine), Mellissa Brown
    (Mathilde Verlaine), Lisa Cohen (Madame Rimbaud)
Narrators: Michael Silverman, Laurence Enjolras, Leslie Thornton,
    Barry Ellsworth, Robert Manenti, Todd Haynes
41 min.

Superstar: The Karen Carpenter Story (1988)
Production: Iced Tea Productions
Director, Writer, and Producer: Todd Haynes
Writer and Producer: Cynthia Schneider
Collaborators: Barry Ellsworth, Robert Manenti
Voice Actors: Merrill Gruver (Karen), Michael Edwards (Richard),
    Melissa Brown (Mother), Rob LaBelle (Mr. A&M / Father),
    Nannie Doyle (Cherry), Cynthia Schneider (Dionne), Larry Kole
    (Announcer)
43 min.

Disappearer (1991)
Music video for Sonic Youth
4 min.

Poison (1991)
Production: Bronze Eye Productions / Arnold A. Semler
Director, Writer ("inspired by the novels of Jean Genet"), and Editor:
   Todd Haynes
Producer: Christine Vachon
Directors of Photography: Maryse Alberti, Barry Ellsworth
Editor: James Lyons
Music: James Bennett
Production Designer: Sarah Stollman
Cast: Edith Meeks (Felicia Beacon), Scott Renderer (John Broom),
   Larry Maxwell (Dr. Graves), Susan Gayle Norman (Nancy Olsen),
   James Lyons (Jack Bolton)
83 min.

Dottie Gets Spanked (1993)
Production: Independent TV Service
Director and Writer: Todd Haynes
Producers: Christine Vachon, Lauren Zalaznick
Director of Photography: Maryse Alberti
Editor: James Lyons
Music: James Bennett
Production Designer: Thérèse Deprez
Cast: Evan Bonifant (Steven Gale), Barbara Garrick (Lorraine Gale),
   Julie Halston (Dottie Frank), Robert Paul (Steven's Father)
27 min.

Safe (1995)
Production: Good Machine / Kardana Productions / Channel 4 Films /
   Arnold Semler
Director and Writer: Todd Haynes
Producers: Christine Vachon, Lauren Zalaznick
Director of Photography: Alex Nepomniaschy
Editor: James Lyons
Music: Ed Tomney
Production Designer: David Bomba
Cast: Julianne Moore (Carol), Peter Friedman (Peter Dunning),
   Xander Berkeley (Greg), Susan Norman (Linda), Kate McGregor Stewart
   (Claire)
121 min.

Velvet Goldmine (1998)
Production: Zenith Productions / Killer Films / Single Cell Pictures
Director and Writer: Todd Haynes
Producer: Christine Vachon
Director of Photography: Maryse Alberti
Editor and Story: James Lyons
Music: Carter Burwell
Production Designer: Christopher Hobbs
Cast: Ewan McGregor (Curt Wild), Jonathan Rhys Meyers (Brian Slade),
    Toni Collette (Mandy Slade), Christian Bale (Arthur Stuart), Eddie Izzard
    (Jerry Devine), Emily Woof (Shannon), Michael Feast (Cecil)
117 min.

Far from Heaven (2002)
Production: Focus Features / Vulcan Productions / Killer Films / John Wells /
    Section Eight
Director and Writer: Todd Haynes
Producers: Jody Patton, Christine Vachon
Director of Photography: Edward Lachman
Editor: James Lyons
Music: Elmer Bernstein
Production Designer: Mark Friedberg
Cast: Julianne Moore (Cathy Whitaker), Dennis Quaid (Frank Whitaker),
    Dennis Haysbert (Raymond Deagan), Patricia Clarkson (Eleanor Fine),
    Viola Davis (Sybil), James Rebhorn (Dr. Bowman), Celia Weston
    (Mona Lauder)
107 min.

I'm Not There (2007)
Production: Killer Films / VIP Media Group / The Weinstein Company /
    Endgame Entertainment / John Wells / John Goldwyn / Rising Star /
    Grey Water Park Productions
Director, Writer, and Story ("inspired by the music and many lives of
    Bob Dylan"): Todd Haynes
Writer: Oren Moverman
Producers: Christine Vachon, James D. Stern, John Sloss, John Goldwyn
Director of Photography: Edward Lachman
Editor: Jay Rabinowitz
Production Designer: Judy Becker
Cast: Christian Bale (Jack / Pastor John), Cate Blanchett (Jude),
    Marcus Carl Franklin (Woody / Chaplin Boy), Richard Gere (Billy),
    Heath Ledger (Robbie), Ben Whishaw (Arthur), Charlotte Gainsbourg
    (Claire), Bruce Greenwood (Keenan Jones / Garrett)
135 min.

Mildred Pierce (2011)

Production: HBO Miniseries / Metro-Goldwyn-Mayer / Killer Films /
    John Wells
Director and Writer (adapted from James M. Cain's novel): Todd Haynes
Writer: Jon Raymond
Director of Photography: Ed Lachman
Editors: Affonso Gonçalves, Camilla Toniolo
Music: Carter Burwell
Production Designer: Mark Friedberg
Cast: Kate Winslet (Mildred Pierce), Evan Rachel Wood (Teenage
    Veda Pierce), Guy Pearce (Monty Beragon), Melissa Leo (Lucy Gessler),
    Brían F. O'Byrne (Bert Pierce), James LeGros (Wally Burgan),
    Mare Winningham (Ida Corwin), Morgan Turner (Young Veda Pierce),
    Hope Davis (Mrs. Forrester)
329 min.

DVD Director Commentaries

Dottie Gets Spanked (Zeitgeist Films, 2004).
Far from Heaven (Universal, 2003).
I'm Not There (Weinstein Company, 2008).
Mildred Pierce (HBO Home Entertainment, 2012).
Poison (Zeitgeist Films, 2011).
Safe (Tartan Video, U.K., 2003).
Velvet Goldmine (Blu-ray, Miramax / Lionsgate, 2011)

Screenplays

Far from Heaven, Safe, Superstar: The Karen Carpenter Story—Three Screen-
plays (New York: Grove Press, 2003).
Velvet Goldmine (London: Faber and Faber, 1998).

Soundtrack Albums

Far from Heaven. Composed, conducted, and produced by Elmer Bernstein.
Varèse Sarabande, 2002.
I'm Not There. Produced by Randall Poster, Jim Dunbar, and Todd Haynes.
Columbia / Sony Music Soundtrax, 2007.
Mildred Pierce. Composed, orchestrated, conducted, and produced by Carter
Burwell. Varèse Sarabande, 2011.
Safe. Composed, arranged, performed, and produced by Ed Tomney. Mute
Records, 1995.
Velvet Goldmine. Produced by Randall Poster, Todd Haynes, and Michael Stipe.
London Records, 1998.

Other Works Cited

Althusser, Louis. "Freud and Lacan." Trans. Ben Brewster. In *Lenin and Philosophy and Other Essays.* London: NLB, 1971. 189–220.

Artaud, Antonin. "On Suicide." Trans. David Rattray. In *Artaud Anthology.* Ed. Jack Hirschman. San Francisco: City Lights, 1965. 56–59.

———. "Van Gogh: The Man Suicided by Society." Trans. Mary Beach and Lawrence Ferlinghetti. In *Artaud Anthology.* Ed. Jack Hirschman. San Francisco: City Lights, 1965. 135–63.

Atwood, Margaret. *The Handmaid's Tale.* New York: Vintage, 1996.

Badiou, Alain. *The Meaning of Sarkozy.* Trans. David Fernbach. London: Verso, 2008.

"Behind the Glam and the Glitter." Velvet Goldmine Making-of Documentary. Film 4 DVD ed., 1998.

Bersani, Leo. *Homos.* Cambridge, Mass.: Harvard University Press, 1995.

———. "Illegitimacy." Unpublished lecture. Communicating Forms: Aesthetics, Relationality, Collaboration conference, University of Chicago, October 21, 2010. In the author's possession.

———. "Is the Rectum a Grave?" (1987). In *Is the Rectum a Grave? and Other Essays.* Chicago: University of Chicago Press, 2010. 3–30.

Bracewell, Michael. *Roxy: The Band That Invented an Era.* London: Faber and Faber, 2007.

Cain, James M. *Mildred Pierce.* 1941; reprint, London: Phoenix, 2011.

Crimp, Douglas. "Mourning and Militancy." *October* 51 (Winter 1989): 3–18.

Davis, Glyn. *Superstar: The Karen Carpenter Story.* London: Wallflower Press, 2008.

Deleuze, Gilles. "Coldness and Cruelty." Trans. Jean McNeil. In *Masochism.* 1967; reprint, New York: Zone Books, 1989. 9–138.

Deleuze, Gilles, and Félix Guattari. *Anti-Oedipus: Capitalism and Schizophrenia.* Trans. Robert Hurley, Mark Seem, and Helen R. Lane. 1972; reprint, London: Athlone Press, 1990.

Doane, Mary Anne. *The Desire to Desire: The Woman's Film of the 1940s.* Bloomington: Indiana University Press, 2008.

Doggett, Peter. *The Man Who Sold the World: David Bowie and the 1970s.* London: Bodley Head, 2011.

Dyer, Richard. Interview with Todd Haynes. Tate Modern, London, June 4, 2004. *Film Studies for Free.* July 4, 2010; accessed July 5, 2012. filmstudiesforfree.blogspot.com/2010/07/on-todd-haynes-happy-independence-day.html.

Dylan, Bob. *Chronicles: Volume One.* London: Pocket Books, 2004.

———. *Tarantula.* 1971; reprint, London: Harper Perennial, 2005.

Fassbinder, Rainer Werner. "Imitation of Life: On the Films of Douglas Sirk." In *The Anarchy of the Imagination: Interviews, Essays, Notes.* Ed. Michael Töteberg and Leo A. Lensing. Trans. Krishna Winston. Baltimore: Johns Hopkins University Press, 1992. 77–89.

Foucault, Michel. *The History of Sexuality, Volume 1: An Introduction.* Trans. Robert Hurley. 1976; reprint, Harmondsworth, Middlesex: Penguin, 1990.

Freud, Sigmund. "'A Child Is Being Beaten' (A Contribution to the Study of the Origin of Sexual Perversions)" (1919). In *The Standard Edition of the Complete Psychological Works of Sigmund Freud.* Vol. 17. Ed. and trans. James Strachey. London: Hogarth Press, 1955. 179–204.

Genet, Jean. Interview for *Arena*, BBC (1985). Accessed July 5, 2012. www .youtube.com/watch?v=uErIxrSX8YI.

Halliday, Jon. *Sirk on Sirk: Conversations with Jon Halliday.* Rev ed. London: Faber and Faber, 1997.

Hay, Louise L. *You Can Heal Your Life.* 1984; reprint, London: Hay House, 2006.

Haynes, Todd. Preface to *Glam! Bowie, Bolan, and the Glitter Rock Revolution,* by Barney Hoskyns. London: Faber and Faber, 1998. x-xi.

———. Video interview about *Fear Eats the Soul.* Arrow DVD edition, 2006.

———. Video introduction to *Le Plaisir.* Criterion DVD edition, 2008.

Hilderbrand, Lucas. "Grainy Days and Mondays: *Superstar* and Bootleg Aesthetics." *Camera Obscura* 19.3 (2004): 56–91.

Hocquenghem, Guy. *Homosexual Desire.* Trans. Daniella Dangoor. 1972; reprint, Durham, N.C.: Duke University Press, 2006.

———. *The Screwball Asses.* Trans. Noura Wedell. 1973; reprint, Los Angeles: Semiotext(e), 2010.

Hoskyns, Barney. *Glam! Bowie, Bolan, and the Glitter Rock Revolution.* London: Faber and Faber, 1998.

Ibsen, Henrik. *The Doll's House.* In *Four Major Plays.* Trans. James McFarlane and Jens Arup. 1879; reprint, Oxford: Oxford World's Classics, 1998.

Laing, R. D. *The Divided Self: An Existential Study in Sanity and Madness.* 1960; reprint, London: Penguin, 1990.

Marcus, Greil. *Bob Dylan by Greil Marcus: Writings 1968–2010.* London: Faber and Faber, 2010.

———. *The Old, Weird America: The World of Bob Dylan's Basement Tapes.* 1997; reprint, New York: Picador, 2011.

Marqusee, Mike. *Chimes of Freedom: The Politics of Bob Dylan's Art.* New York: New Press, 2003.

Mildred Pierce Home Page. HBO (2012). Accessed July 5, 2012. www.hbo.com/mildred-pierce/index.html.

Miller, Henry. *The Time of the Assassins: A Study of Rimbaud.* 1946; reprint, New York: New Directions, 1962.

Moverman, Oren, ed. "And All Is Well in Our World—Making *Safe*: Todd Haynes, Julianne Moore, and Christine Vachon." In *Projections 5: Filmmakers on Filmmaking.* Ed. John Boorman and Walter Donohue. London: Faber and Faber, 1996. 198–234.

———. "Superstardust: Talking Glam with Todd Haynes." In *Velvet Goldmine,* by Todd Haynes. London: Faber and Faber, 1998. ix–xxxi.

Nietzsche, Friedrich. *Thus Spoke Zarathustra.* Trans. R. J. Hollingdale. 1883–85; reprint, London: Penguin, 1969.

Penley, Constance. *NASA/TREK: Popular Science and Sex in America.* London: Verso, 1997.

Penman, Ian. "The Shattered Glass: Notes on Bryan Ferry." In *Zoot Suits and Second-Hand Dresses: An Anthology of Fashion and Music.* Ed. Angela McRobbie. Basingstoke, Hampshire: Macmillan, 1989. 103–17.

Rechy, John. *The Sexual Outlaw: A Documentary.* 1977; reprint, New York: Grove Press, 1984.

Rich, B. Ruby. "New Queer Cinema." In *New Queer Cinema: A Critical Reader.* Ed. Michele Aaron. Edinburgh: Edinburgh University Press, 2004. 15–22.

Satellite of Love: A Velvet Goldmine Fan Fiction Archive. February 5, 2005; accessed July 5, 2012. satellite.shriftweb.org.

Schlumberger, Hella. "'I've Changed along with the Characters in my Films': A Discussion with Hella Schlumberger about Work and Love, the Exploitability of Feelings, and the Longing for Utopia." In *The Anarchy of the Imagination: Interviews, Essays, Notes.* Ed. Michael Töteberg and Leo A. Lensing. Trans. Krishna Winston. Baltimore: Johns Hopkins University Press, 1992. 16–30.

Schmidt, Randy L. *The Life of Karen Carpenter: Little Girl Blue.* London: Omnibus Press, 2010.

Sedgwick, Eve Kosofsky. "A Poem Is Being Written." *Representations* 17 (Winter 1987): 110–43.

Van Gogh, Vincent. *The Letters of Vincent Van Gogh.* Ed. Ronald de Leeuw. Trans. Arnold Pomerans. London: Penguin, 1997.

Varda the Message. *Velvet Goldmine* Fan Site. Accessed July 5, 2012. vardathemessage.tumblr.com.

White, Rob. "Long and Grinding Road: *No Direction Home: Bob Dylan." Sight and Sound* (November 2005): 92.

Williams, Linda. "Melancholy Melodrama: Almodovarian Grief and Lost Homosexual Attachments." In *All About Almodóvar.* Ed. Brad Epps and Despina Kakoudaki. Minneapolis: University of Minnesota Press, 2009. 166–92.

Wyatt, Justin. "Cinematic/Sexual Transgression: An Interview with Todd Haynes." *Film Quarterly* 46.3 (Summer 1993): 2–8.

Rob White, the editor of *Film Quarterly,* is the author
of *Freud's Memory: Psychoanalysis, Mourning
and the Foreign Body* and the BFI Film
Classics study on *The Third Man.*

Books in the series
Contemporary Film Directors

Philip Kaufman
  Annette Insdorf

Richard Linklater
  David T. Johnson

David Lynch
  Justus Nieland

John Sayles
  David R. Shumway

Dario Argento
  L. Andrew Cooper

Todd Haynes
  Rob White

The University of Illinois Press
is a founding member of the
Association of American University Presses.

Designed by Paula Newcomb
Composed in 10/13 New Caledonia LT Std
with Helvetica Neue LT Std display
by Celia Shapland
at the University of Illinois Press
Manufactured by Thomson-Shore, Inc.

University of Illinois Press
1325 South Oak Street
Champaign, IL 61820-6903
www.press.uillinois.edu